I have known Jim Powell since his sem
that he is a wise, godly, courageous,
His experience in faithful, fruitful t
much to teach us all. May the Lord use this book to inspire and
equip many other local pastors—at home and abroad—to be
Boldly Bi-Vocational.

Douglas A. Sweeney
Dean and Professor of Divinity, Beeson Divinity School
Birmingham, Alabama

Having spent several seasons in bi-vocational ministry myself,
I deeply resonate with Jim's reflections and biblical insights on
his pastoral journey. Without romanticizing his experience, he
highlights the strategic gospel opportunities that bi-vocational
ministry offers both pastors and churches. In the rapidly
secularizing West, this vision for ministry will only grow in
relevance and importance.

Kevin Walker
Director of Ministries, The Charles Simeon Trust

Jim Powell has made an excellent contribution to the field of
pastoral ministry. In a day when more and more churches have
less and less people, providing the funding for a "full-time" pastor
may be impossible. *Boldly Bi-Vocational* provides these churches
with exciting new strategies for bridging the financial gap with
tent-making options. This is a must read for churches, pastors,
and church-planters!

William J. Curtis
Lead Pastor, Cornerstone Baptist Church
Darlington, South Carolina

Boldly Bi-Vocational is a gift to the church. In these pages, Jim
Powell presents a biblically grounded and practically-applied
vision for pastoral ministry. This book should be required reading

for all seminary students and church leaders. Jim's words have deeply encouraged me to continue to use my gifts to pursue a singular calling to make the Gospel known wherever God has placed me. It is my prayer that many others will respond to this call to experience the "wonder and adventure" of the bi-vocational life!

Josh Kwasny
Certified EOS Implementer®;
Pastor of Soma Valley Church in Lewisville, NC

Boldly Bi-Vocational is a clarion call for pastors serving their communities. Jim Powell's plea to assess the opportunities and costs that await those who see their engagement in the marketplace as part of their pastoral call is imperative. Everyone considering ministry or who is ordained should wrestle through this work to gain greater clarity on what it means to serve Christ in their community.

CHRIS VOGEL
Church Planting and Vitality Coordinator
Mission to North America, Presbyterian Church in America

As Christians, we each seek to honor Christ as we walk and serve in the different callings where God has placed us. In *Boldly Bi-Vocational*, Jim shares practical insights on a ministry model which can be a gift specifically for pastors. In a sense, a gift of freedom to think differently about the gospel ministry. One can be effective in the call of pastoring God's sheep while also living more in the world around them that does not know the church or the light of the gospel. Not letting *Boldly Bi-Vocational* challenge your view of ministry may be a missed opportunity to experience new passion and energy, and overall effectiveness, in the work of bringing light to a people who walk in darkness.

MARK HECHT
Founder, Coaching Horizons

CHRISTIAN
FOCUS

Unless otherwise stated the Scripture quotations are from The Holy Bible, English Standard Version, copyright © 2001 by Crossway Bibles, a publishing ministry of Good News Publishers. Used by permission. All rights reserved.

Copyright © James M. Powell 2025

paperback ISBN 978-1-5271-1226-1
ebook ISBN 978-1-5271-1310-7

10 9 8 7 6 5 4 3 2 1

Published in 2025

by

Christian Focus Publications Ltd.,
Geanies House, Fearn, Ross-shire
IV20 1TW, Great Britain.

www.christianfocus.com

Cover design by Rhian Muir

Printed and bound by
Bell and Bain Glasgow

MIX
Paper | Supporting
responsible forestry
FSC® C007785
FSC
www.fsc.org

All rights reserved. No part of this publication may be reproduced, stored in a retrieval system, or transmitted, in any form, by any means, electronic, mechanical, photocopying, recording or otherwise without the prior permission of the publisher or a licence permitting restricted copying. In the U.K. such licences are issued by the Copyright Licensing Agency, 4 Battlebridge Lane, London, SE1 2HX www.cla.co.uk

For Kori and LMNOPQ –

together in this undivided life.

Contents

Foreword

I read Jim Powell's *Boldly Bi-Vocational* through in one sitting. Cover to cover. And not from obligation. I was curious at first, then intrigued, as the initial chapters sped by. Finally, fascinated, challenged and genuinely excited about the biblical argument he makes in this book.

Boldly Bi-Vocational had me thinking about Amos, the ancient prophet, and men like him today. I suspect Amos could have used a copy of this book, had it been published in his day. For he knew all too well the experiential realities of bi-vocational ministry. Not much is known about Amos, other than that he hailed from the rural village of Tekoa, located about five miles south-east of Bethlehem. And that he was a herder of sheep before he became a shepherd over God's household. If his "full time" job with flocks wasn't reason enough to keep from becoming bi-vocational, Amos was a farmer as well (we are told that he had some sycamore trees that required his attention). Amos, like many of you getting ready to read this book, knew the daily grind of work. In his case, handling unruly flocks needing food in rugged terrain while holding down another job. To put it simply, when Amos was called into to a season of preaching, he already had a vocation. And then some. And they took all his time. Until, that is, God called him (just like he calls many today who can relate to him) to give himself to both the Word and his other work.

Jim Powell writes for just such men. Rugged men. Rural men. (And yes, even men who find themselves already well situated and financially resourced.) Rather than rehearse the argument Jim will make in the pages that follow, I simply want to highlight three aspects of the book that I found downright compelling. First, the author himself. Powell writes with positive ethos – that is to say, he has credibility. He has done this. Much of it is first person stuff. And what's more, I am reminded that Jim entered the bi-vocational life in ways that most don't. He was a full-time pastor first. As a result, he has a lot to offer men who have labored long in bi-vocational settings hoping to shed the label altogether. Second, the book makes a compelling case – from the Bible – that bi-vocational ministry is not something done only from necessity, as though a calling less than desirable. Instead, the book is out to prove that one should consider adopting the model boldly, that is – by choice – by a freedom of the will borne out of a deep love for the gospel. Finally, Powell treats the challenges, as well as prospects, of choosing to become bi-vocational in a straightforward manner. He neither glamorizes the method, nor does he shy from helping you count the costs before diving in.

This book will be a great encouragement to men among us already serving in bi-vocational settings. It will bolster your confidence. And dare I say, it will help you learn to boast in your calling. And for those of us who end up remaining in traditional settings, this book will set your heart ablaze with admiration for the men God is choosing to honor with this work. I am grateful that Jim wrote it. I have learned much from this man who has a foot in two worlds – the church and the workplace. Enjoy!

David R. Helm
Senior Pastor, Christ Church Chicago
Chairman, The Charles Simeon Trust

Preface

For more than a decade, I served as a pastor or church planter within a traditional model of ministry. Through a series of providences, I was led to voluntarily step outside of the familiar and "normal" and to live out my calling as a tentmaker. This began a journey that has morphed into a bold bi-vocationalism as I have grown convinced of the biblical permission as well as the strategic impact of such a life.

I will never forget the Charles Simeon Trust preaching workshop in Providence, Rhode Island during May 2022. While serving as an Instructor, I was peppered with questions by a local pastor over lunch about the specifics of my story and convictions. "How are you here as a preaching instructor, serving as the lead/teaching pastor of a multi-pastor church, and also serving bi-vocationally in your local community? How does that work?" I understood the reason for his inquiry. Sitting around us were ministers from small churches across New England, many of whom he felt might be encouraged to think differently about a tentmaking or bi-vocational paradigm. Most, as he saw it, viewed bi-vocational ministry as a necessity to be endured, hurried to a terminus as soon as a pastor was able to transition to "full-time ministry." He was convinced I needed to speak up about it, if for no other reason than to share an alternative vision. This brother confidently and repeatedly (through later emails) asked me to *write about it*. However, the busyness of being a husband and father of six as well as the responsibility-laden life of bi-vocationalism prevented me from writing anything. Ironically, my "other" vocation is … writing. I contract for housing nonprofits to write grants and to manage a team who facilitates corporate and foundation partnerships. Functionally, I had no time to write about being intentionally bi-vocational. I was too busy doing it.

I have read that C.S. Lewis, though he received countless requests to write on a myriad of subjects, would not pen a word unless he had something to say. This is humility and wisdom. While I, in no way, have his humility, wisdom or writing acumen – I have come to believe that the Lord has given me something to say (beyond the local church pulpit). Having now served in this complex ministry paradigm for more than a decade, I have acquiesced and given my best attempt to write a few words that I trust help drive the conversation forward that the church should be having about biblical modes and models of ministry. As I surrendered to trying to write about what I had been doing, I quickly discovered that there was a bigger discussion happening across denominations and church planting networks about the validity of bi-vocational and multi-vocational ministry. I had no idea, as my head was to the ground in my local community.

A bi-vocational life is full of wonder and adventure. It is a boastworthy calling. It is a missionary life. It is complex, with vast opportunity cost. In the pages that follow, I will consider the biblical merits of this life, providing personal reflection even as I unashamedly seek to persuade you toward, or encourage you in, this model. I will humbly propose it as a biblical, necessary consideration for the church in all places and cultures – *especially the spaces where* ministry has been professionalized to the point that tentmaking and bi-vocational ministry are hardly thought of as something to "boast in" (1 Cor. 9:15). I will offer it to you as a strategic, transferable model of localized, gift-utilizing ministry for the church both in modern and upper-middle class cultures in the West, as well as in hard-to-serve places around the world. It is my desire that each reader can evaluate and consider this model as relates to his own church reality, community context, personal gift set, and family capacity.

If you are bi-vocational in your current ministry role – I hope you read all of these pages. You are doing this, and I want to encourage you. You are in the pipeline of God's provision and grace! I would have much I could learn from you were we to swap stories. Thanks be to God for His provision and His Word that informs us of this model! Celebrate your unique calling and trust the God who has equipped you for it and who provides for you through it. If you are bi-vocational-by-necessity and you long to serve the church "full-time" in a traditional ministry model, please understand – your season in this iteration of your calling is not Plan B! It is God's design for you for as long as He calls you to it. He has equipped you for this assignment, and He will deploy you through it to represent His kingdom in your local community. May these pages help you boast in the ministry model that you employ in your assigned sphere of influence (2 Cor. 10:13)! May no one – not even yourself – "deprive you" of your "ground for boasting" (1 Cor. 9:15) as you navigate a sacrificial, complex and wonderful assignment from God.

Whether you are an urban church planter or a rural pastor of a small congregation, I encourage you to consider bi-vocationalism or even bonafide "tentmaking" as a valid, strategic, biblical model of ministry that is worthy of bold pursuit. If you are not a pastor or missionary but serve as an elder or leader in the local church, I sincerely hope you will be catalysed to brainstorm how you might release your local church leaders to creatively fulfil the mission of Christ and his church from within *any* biblically authorized framework. To that end, I commend to you an intentional, bold bi-vocational paradigm.

James M. Powell

Tenets and Commitments

As you read, I offer these important tenets and theological commitments that have guided my work. I expect that they are not violated, directly or by inference, in the pages that follow.

1. God has revealed His sovereign design for creation and redemption in His inerrant, infallible, inspired Word.

2. Every paradigm for individual and ecclesiastical ministry must be grounded in the Word of God in order for it to be sanctioned by God and legitimate to His ends.

3. A biblically authorized paradigm for ministry and the application of that paradigm are not the same thing.

4. No construct of ministry has the power to bring the kingdom of heaven down to earth, such that hearts are changed, sinners are saved, and the kingdom advances.

5. The Spirit of God applying the Word of God by means of the preached gospel of God about the work of the Son of God is alone able to accomplish these ends, according to God's sovereign design and for His glory.

6. Creativity and flexibility within the boundaries of the declared will of God is to the glory of God and will be used by God. Creativity, originality and ingenuity outside of the

revealed Word of God is not to be celebrated, pursued, nor expected to be effective.

7. Every individual servant of God, as well as the local church established by God, has been given an assigned sphere of influence by God (2 Cor. 10:13), and thus is unique in their capacity and giftedness, equipped to represent the kingdom of Jesus and to glorify God within that time and space.

8. The influence of the church of God in the assigned sphere of influence established by God must occur within the authority structures established by the Word of God – namely church elders. In light of this commitment, in the pages that follow, a complementarian interpretation of the office of elder (pastor) will be utilized and grammatically reflected.

9. Individuals and churches must contextualize each biblical model of ministry which they may be suited to employ – evangelizing the local community and discipling members of the church where God has placed them.

Introduction

Isn't This Something Missionaries Often Do?

During the process of writing this book I have often needed to explain what bi-vocational and tentmaking ministry are, both to those who are churched and unchurched. These are usually enjoyably perplexing conversations, especially with the unchurched, as all manner of theological realities are connected. In most of these dialogues – especially with those who are familiar with the Bible, the church, and the kingdom of Jesus – I am asked about foreign missionaries.

"So, is your book for missionaries? Don't a lot of missionaries do that?"

Yes, this is a book for missionaries. And yes, many foreign missionaries are tentmakers in the region where they have been sent. It is not uncommon for missionaries to "do business" while on mission in a foreign culture. In fact, particularly in places that are closed to Christianity, a missionary's vocation often legalizes their presence. This is of redemptive design and has been potently utilized for the glory of God and the spread of His gospel! In His sovereign providence, God has often orchestrated secular vocational assignments as a means of positioning His servants across His world for the glorious mission of His kingdom.

While it is not my intent to focus on foreign missions or to propose how tentmaking or bi-vocational ministry could be effective in cross-cultural contexts, I do expect that this book will resonate with missionaries who live outside of their natural culture and context. In fact, the presentation of a bigger vision of bi-vocationalism flows, in part, out of my observation of foreign missionaries.

When considering that "many missionaries do this" it is worthy of clarifying variegated models. While some indeed *are* vocationally employed in a business out "in the field," in reality, their material needs are not directly connected to that vocation. Rather, they are dominantly or even fully provided for by God through the church in the West (or elsewhere) and their vocation is a missions outpost disconnected from their material provision. Financially, they operate within a more traditional missionary model. Their local employment is primarily a "cover" for their missionary engagement, establishing their legal presence. While the type of business is expectantly strategic for bringing the kingdom of heaven into the kingdom of this world, by which the gospel might be shared and presented to individuals through it – it is not a business upon which their material support depends. This is not uncommon, and it is wonderful.

I have spent time, dominantly in Asia, with foreign missionaries who were explicit that their vocation was a cover, instructing me in the specifics and the semantics of their industry so that I could justify my role should I be interrogated as to my (short-term) presence. In other words, some miss-ionaries hold a vocation, not so much for God to provide for their material needs, but so that they can be there in the first place. This both legitimates their long-term locality even as it enables them to grow trusted relationships with locals for the expanding of God's kingdom. This is glorious and of God's design – and through it the Lord has formed relationships that have introduced people to Jesus, producing disciples and planting churches. *Soli Deo gloria*!

This is different, however, than a tentmaking missionary in a closed country who works in a trade or business that provides all of their material support (or if bi-vocational – partial material support). Their secular employment may indeed enable their legal presence, but it also makes it financially possible to remain in the field. Not to mention, it removes the financial burden from "sending" churches. It is often strategic for a missionary to begin with "missions support" in hopes of transitioning to partial or full business income. This is worthy of emphasis and emulation. Consider the impact in an impoverished third-world country, when, not only is a missionary provided for but their business provides for dozens or hundreds of local employees and their families. May God alone receive the glory! My point being – their vocation is not a cover. It is a strategic cultural and economic influencer, even as it functions as the core source of provision from God. Allow me to repeat myself: this is of God's providential design! Through it the Lord has formed relationships that have introduced people to Jesus, producing disciples and planting churches. *Soli Deo gloria*!

This latter model of tentmaking missions is more akin to the tentmaking and bi-vocationalism described in the pages that follow. In fact, what follows is an attempt to persuade the church in the West to embrace a bold vision for a model of ministry that has most often – or, most visibly – been deployed by international missionaries in difficult foreign contexts.

During the season of my own paradigm shift from traditional ministry into tentmaking and bi-vocationalism (which will be described in chapter 1), I was privileged to make multiple trips to Asia to help lead preaching workshops with the Charles Simeon Trust. While the purpose of my travel was to instruct indigenous pastors and church planters, I also took the opportunity to visit multiple missionaries from the West that were supported by my local church. These families were living out both of the previously mentioned iterations of business-as-missions. I was struck by the intention and intensity of their philosophies of ministry, by their courage amidst the threat of persecution, and by their confidence in the providence of God to use them in the sphere of influence to which they had been assigned.

During those trips, I became enamored with the potency of the mission of God through servants whom He culturally positioned and assigned in local trades or businesses. They were vocational missionaries, poised and ready to share the gospel, but I was struck by how their leadership and strategic mindedness was not solely "as a missionary" but also as a community-impacting business owner or leader. They were strategic creators of vibrant businesses – with business plans, ethics, cultures and products that reflected the glory of God the creator and redeemer. They had been deployed by God to provide for the material needs of their employees, even as they presented the gospel and formed worship gatherings of those whom the Lord converted. It was a multi-faceted, multi-sectored investment. They were not just "missionaries who happened to be connected to a business" (for legal or other purposes), they were missionaries leading or owning businesses that were impacting their local economy and the fabric of the social culture that visibly needed redemption – fair wages, honorable treatment of laborers, justice and mercy.

A HOLY AGITATION

On each flight back to the States, I felt a holy agitation for multiple reasons. First, I was stunned by having met so many local pastors who were provided for by God through tentmaking or some bi-vocational construct. Most of the pastors who attended the preaching workshops had sacrificed daily wages so that they might be trained in how to faithfully handle the Word of God. These brothers worked tremendously long hours in a variety of jobs that they might support their families, even as they pastored house churches. These pastors were not professionals. They were sacrificial, hardworking, persecution-enduring ministers of the gospel. Moved as I was by the intentionality of these pastors who were living out of an entirely different paradigm than I had known – at the same time, I was equally moved by my exposure to missionaries who lived like pastors, yet who were functional laypersons, owning or operating businesses.

The dual exposure to a culture of dominantly tentmaking or bi-vocational pastors (and their churches) as well as to secularly employed missionaries was overwhelming. I trembled writing notes in my journal on the flight home.

My heart raced as I thought about the kingdom of God. Honestly, it felt very different than what I had known in the church in the West. I deeply knew it. This is exactly how every layperson is to live out their discipleship of Jesus in their places of employment in a secular world. Every disciple of Jesus – whether employed by a corporation, school, hospital, nonprofit, or self-employed – ought to function as a tentmaking missionary where God has placed them.

But do they? Do we, as the visible church (again, mostly in the West – whether in urban, suburban or rural places), visibly evidence this culture among our laypersons? Is it the norm? I began to pray for my friends and congregant laypersons back home. Was their grid of life and purpose as potent and culturally invasive as I had just observed? How would I, as their pastor and preacher, call them to a missionary life more than I thought I already was doing?

Between fits of turbulence on the long flights, I journaled disparate thoughts. I thought about the apostle Paul and his tentmaking. He was a businessman and a missionary; a missionary who ran a business. And yet, Paul was not a layperson. He was an *Apostle* – a uniquely "chosen instrument" of Jesus, called to carry His name before the nations, kings and the children of Israel (Acts 9:16). Paul was a church planter who trained elders. He discipled pastors. He was less like a missionary layperson and more like a tentmaking pastor!

I felt myself spiritually hyperventilating at the thought of my own calling.

The seed was in the ground. Perhaps it had been so for some time. It was being watered and the sun was shining down.

Since that time, more than a decade ago, the seed of tentmaking and bi-vocational ministry has been watered by the Word and begun to grow. Providentially, God has brought indigenous assignments in my own life and sustained my family through it. It has become my way of life as a pastor, straddling worlds in ways I could not have imagined when I was first called to ministry (more on calling in chapter 2).

Boldly Bi-vocational is my small contribution to a world of words. Many pastors, theologians, and missionaries have already competently and clearly written about the themes I will address. However, I believe that this kingdom topic is worthy of a few more. The church of Jesus is called unceasingly to bring the gospel to the communities where God has placed us, and I am convinced that a bold bi-vocationalism can be an unheralded means to that end – both in domestic and foreign missions contexts. What would be the kingdom impact in our communities if more ministers of the gospel were enabled to steward their *primary and best gifts* in both the church and community around the church – not as a financial stopgap, but as a fulfilling, full-time model of ministry that is their "ground of boasting" (1 Cor. 9:15)? What could be the impact within corporations, schools, nonprofits, or government? More so, how might this bring balance and emboldened mission to the minister and his family? How might it unburden the local church, profoundly emphasize local missions, and lead to the adoption of a biblical, team-approach to ministry (rather than leaning on "jack of all trades" or dangerously orbiting around celebrity pastors)?

These are the questions that *Boldly Bi-Vocational* will pose and seek to answer.

Part One

FIRST THINGS

1

Ministry Burnout and a Paradigm Shift

Teach me your way, O Lord,
that I may walk in your truth;
unite my heart to fear your name.
—Psalm 86:11

"I am not burnt out. I am just tired and this is just ministry." It was 2013 and I felt like a vacuum had sucked up all of my energy. Gone.

I will always remember *that* dinner when my wife and I met with an elder and his wife from the church where I had served as church planter for seven years. We intimately discussed my looming transition, as I had recently resigned to pursue a tentmaking model of ministry in a different region of the country. I was leaving.

After an awkward pause, words were shared with me that I wish I could unhear. "You can't leave. You are the energy of the church."

Silence.

She was not wrong. But it was all wrong. No faithful pastor or church planting missionary should want to receive that description of their ministry. The pastor is never to be the energy of a local church. Ever. That is the role of the Spirit of God alone. No wonder I was burnt out.

I had spent more than a decade as a solo pastor and church planter, both in rural and suburban metropolitan contexts. My ministry experiences, by the grace of God, had been fruitful with visible congregational growth and maturing. Truly, the previous seven years in which our family had surrendered to a call to plant a reformed, evangelical church in Emmaus, Pennsylvania had been hard, but beautiful. I understood the sorrow and angst of this elder and his wife.

I had the undeserved honor of serving as the catalyst and shepherd of a congregation that the Lord had sustainably planted in a region of the country that *needed* healthy churches. The depressed and secularized metropolitan area needed churches that would shamelessly herald Christ and Him crucified with leaders functioning within a biblical polity, who remained committed to the simple means of grace (Word and sacrament), and who evidenced that weakness "is the way" for the power of Christ to be known among us (2 Cor. 12:9). Over those seven years, I had tried to live out a simple philosophy of ministry that orbited around the exposition of God's Word, both in corporate worship and in communal gatherings. In God's kindness, a fledgling and yet sustainable church was formed with a visible love of the Word, genuine relationships, minimal programs, and an intergenerational vibe with many young families, empty nesters and college students.

GOD WAS PLANTING A CHURCH,
I WAS BURNING OUT

I was in my thirties. My wife and I had four children at the time and, through every step of the journey, I wrestled with my immaturity as a husband, father and disciple – while pastoring, alone. It was a time of immense self-exposure. By God's grace, I was always perplexed, but never crushed. The calling and mercy of God were simultaneously confirmed, time and again. I felt as if Paul's words were directly to me: [J]imothy, "practice these things, immerse yourself in them, so that all may see your progress. Keep a close watch on yourself and on the teaching. Persist in this, for by so doing you will save both yourself and your hearers" (1 Tim. 4:15-16). I was making progress, and God was undoubtedly "saving me" through the very calling He had placed on my life to preach the gospel.

And yet, I was still somehow oblivious to the risk and instability of my ministry rhythms. I was expending ridiculous amounts of mental and physical energy. *My* energy. Like many church planters and pastors, I was consumed by it. I would fixate on failures, hopes, plans, and the words of people.

I recall a painful visit to Central Park on a day trip to New York City with our extended family. It was literally painful. While my kids ran and played, I lay down in the grass seeking relief for my stomach pain. I was trying to turn it off. Trying to unplug. But I did not know how. Something was very wrong in my life of vocational ministry. It stayed wrong for multiple years, try as I would to fix it.

While God was graciously planting a church, I was burning out.

Fast-forward back to *that* dinner. Nine months before that evening, the Lord brought me through a crucial ministry moment that He used to produce a seismic change. I was preaching through 1 Corinthians during the Fall of 2012. It was late October, the very week that Hurricane Sandy pummelled the Northeast. For multiple days our home was without power or heat, so our family camped in the living room near the fire. I would stay up into the middle of each night, working on my sermon while stoking the fire. That first night, I kept reading 1 Corinthians 9, my preaching text. I was sleepless and churning. After the second night, the scribbles in my journal produced more than a preaching outline. While I knew that the main argument of the text for my sermon was that *"for the sake of the gospel" we who are in Christ must deny our rights* (become all things to all people that by any means God would save them through the good news of Jesus who gave up His rights) – for my own life, the messy pages of my journal evidenced a more acute application. I immediately and firmly sensed a call to a different model of ministry.

In the early part of 1 Corinthians 9, the Apostle Paul uses his own vocational life as an example of giving up his rights. "If we sow spiritual things among you, do we not have a right to reap material benefit?" He makes it clear that it is a right – designed by God – that a minister of the gospel receive material and financial support from those he serves. "But I have made no use of any of these rights – for I would rather die than have anyone deprive me of my ground for boasting" (1 Cor. 9:15). It struck me. Paul voluntarily gave up ministerial remuneration and he served Christ with freedom. He was not a tentmaking missionary by necessity or for a short term. He was bold and boastful of it as his life calling.

It felt like a hurricane had carried me from a place of familiarity and safety to a place where I had never been, nor planned to be, but where great faith and freedom would grow. Overnight I sensed a call toward a major vocational paradigm shift. The winds of the hurricane outside of my home had faded, but the wind of the Spirit blew within me toward a voluntary change. I was suddenly free to pray for a new construct in ministry that would affect my relationship with all whom I might pastor in the future, and that would change my relationship with the vocation itself. I knew that I had long been unhealthy within the "traditional model" of pastoral ministry. While I appeared bold and confident, even happy, I regularly struggled with oppressive fear of man. Through those years, I regrettably did not have the maturity to pastor with freedom within a framework that positioned me as the leader of a community that I was outside of (yet that paid my salary). I felt trapped. And in an instant, the Holy Spirit used 1 Corinthians 9 to offer a freeing alternative.

THE NINE MONTHS THAT BIRTHED
A NEW PARADIGM

For nine months I churned toward this change. I sought counsel. How does one remain a functional, positioned pastor, while pursuing a tentmaking or bi-vocational model with intention? Where do I start? Burdened yet excited, I called denominational leaders to once again explore church planting in various cities across the country. I shared my conviction (and the condition) that I "just find a job" in a target community, laboring freely unto planting a church. I was zealous not to raise support. Expectantly, nothing matriculated. I applied for corporate jobs in various cities and various sectors. I endured awkward conversations with strangers as I tried to justify how I might benefit their business, even though my resume was filled exclusively with church leadership roles. I was rejected countless times.

I had committed wholesale to a construct of ministry that I had never seen done, nor did it feel possible. But I kept searching.

The hardest conversations were with ministry peers. "So you're quitting?" No. "But you now want to be a part-time pastor?" No. I tried to reiterate that I was the same man and the same pastor with the same gifts whose vision of serving in the kingdom and the church was very much "full-time." I held the same conviction about the local church and the mission of God. I was not quitting.

In God's providence, nine months later, this new paradigm was borne out in my life. I was hired to serve as a full-time Executive Director for a housing nonprofit in South Carolina. Literally, God gave me the opportunity to repair and "make tents" for low-income families. Simultaneously, I was called to serve as an unpaid Associate Pastor at a church plant, where I was given great latitude to navigate a new season of ministry that was completely foreign to what I had known previously. I preached regularly, though not frequently, as well as helped with leadership development in an effort to support the church planting pastor. I learned what it felt like to be an elder who was *not* employed by the church. (This experience alone has been transformative for ministry.) I will be forever grateful to Blythewood Presbyterian Church for putting up with my zeal even as they let me recover from burnout. I was a mess.

To my surprise, with each passing week, I realized just how much I was using the same gift set inside and outside of the church. I observed patterns and behaviors within myself that showed up in *both* places. Some of these observations surprised me, as I had previously assumed that those habits were purely a result of a "professionalized" life of full-time ministry in the local church. Apparently not. I felt keenly aware that I was living a single, undivided life that had been designed by God, though I was functioning in a vocational duality. Suddenly, I found myself dominantly pastoring people outside of the local church, even as I was preaching the Word of God to people within the church.

I had two feet in two worlds, the sacred and the secular, and for the first time in my vocational life I felt... balanced. And I was free. Whether a given week afforded opportunities for preaching and teaching, or for making philanthropic business presentations and board reports to corporate executives – I was the same man, with less burden and more responsibility.

I had not quit. I was still running the race of pastoral ministry, just with a different stride.

COMPARISON: A RUNNER'S JOURNEY

I am an average runner. When I am not injured, I put more than the average weekly miles on my legs for a middle-aged man. As every runner knows, the more one runs, the greater the likelihood for chronic pain or a forced hiatus due to injury. During my thirties, though I could run a half-marathon at a decently fast clip, I was chronically in pain, whether it was my IT band or my plantar fascia. Not long before I entered a tentmaking (and then a bi-vocational) paradigm, I had also made a significant transition to my running stride.

For decades, I had been wearing comfortable running shoes that made me lazy in my stride. With a large, cushioned heel, I became a heel-striker. Unbeknownst to me, every stride was a blow to my body with excessive pounds of pressure per strike. It does not take a degree in Kinesiology to know that God did not design our heels to be shocks. And yet, my stride mechanics really did not concern me much. I was quick enough for an aging runner and running produced real joy. Apparently running made me a nicer husband, father and pastor. But I was hurting myself.

Eventually my bodily pain justified a little research and development toward a new stride. Advice was not hard to find. There are countless authorities that provide recreational runners with oft-contradicting guidance on running shoes, running diet, and running mechanics. I absorbed just enough counsel to make a massive change. Swiftly, I transitioned to barefooted running, risking any number of new pains and potential problems. But something had to change.

There I was, serving as a church planter in the very city where *Runner's World* magazine was published (Emmaus,

Pennsylvania) and I was the shoeless man running down Main Street in the middle of winter wearing 6mm rubber "Jesus sandals." Awkwardly, my highly qualified *Runner's World* neighbors were running by me on the same streets and trails with their expensive running shoes. I had swung the pendulum to the other side.

While I no longer run in sandals, I went through a constellation of changes – an intentional paradigm shift that resulted in different shoes, a different mindset, and different running mechanics. More than a decade after that change, I am healthier and faster. As I now run the streets and trails around Johnson City, Tennessee, my stride looks nothing like it did ten years ago. I was a runner then and I am a runner now. It just looks different.

The point is this. *A paradigm shift necessarily leads to connected adjustments in how one goes about pursuing the same activity, or calling.* I wonder how many church leaders, missionaries and ministers of the gospel need to consider if they are oft-broken by the pressure of ministry not only because ministry is challenging and sin is real, and not only because they are frail and finite, but because something is off in their stride. Perhaps part of the problem is that pastors and their families are running with a gait within a professionalized model of ministry that needs paradigmatic reconsideration.

Over the last two decades, my trajectory of ministry has shifted from the traditional paradigm of a solo-pastor and church planter to a 'boastful' confidence in a boldly bi-vocational model that has redemptively impacted my family, the local church and the community where I live. It has enabled a far more strategic life in the city where I have been called – with a broader sphere of influence. Ironically, it has created a simpler, undivided life. The words of David in Psalm 86:11 have increasingly been my prayer:

Teach me your way, O Lord,
 that I may walk in your truth;
unite my heart to fear your name.

A REVOLUTIONARY KIND OF CHANGE

A paradigm shift is always revolutionary. It goes against the established ways of doing things. As such, it is not easily comprehended by those who are content or effective within the status quo. In my own story, the voluntary shift from a "successful" life of ministry to a fragile and unfamiliar tentmaking (and then bi-vocational) model was revolutionary in my small circle of influence. In many conversations I surprisingly felt like I needed to defend not only my sense of call, but the biblical merits of the model. I was at a point in ministry where I was expected to stay where I was serving and experience growth, or I was told it would have been more understandable if I moved on "to a larger church with a more influential pulpit." Those realities would have required no justification. However, our voluntary transition was plainly outside of the accepted paradigm, and thus it was incomprehensible to many. It was as revolutionary as it has been life-giving and ministry-expanding.

Since making the change, I have been asked many repeat questions from pastors and laypersons. Isn't the normal model of pastoral ministry just fine? Doesn't a purposeful bi-vocational or tentmaking model necessarily (and thus intentionally) divide the attention of the pastor? Shouldn't pastors be paid by the churches they serve and then do just that… serve the people who pay them? If bi-vocationalism is needed to make ends meet, shouldn't it be for as short of a time as possible, to then get back to full-time ministry?

These questions are expected if the current paradigm is comfortable and normal and works well enough. Sadly, many of the questions I was asked had an underlying assumption that to not employ a traditional or professional model of pastoral ministry is to somehow not "fully" be a pastor. "Jim, now remind me… you used to be a pastor, but now you lead charities or something?" Nope. Still a pastor. Full-time, serving Christ and His church with an undivided life, within a biblical framework.

These comments remind me of some of the advice I received during my running-stride revolution. "If it hurts to run … why not just pick up cycling?" Um, because it's not running. And I am a runner.

Bi-vocational ministry is not quitting. It is not part-time. It is not an about-faced pursuit of a corporate life or a secular vocation. It is not purposeful distraction or a necessary dilution of ministry. It is still running. It is still pastoring. Just with a different stride.

A prayer for the bi-vocational minister, to this end.

O Lord who made us in your image and for your glory,
Teach me your way, that I may walk in your truth. Give me an
undivided life that fears your name. Protect me from the delusion of
a categorical existence and forgive me for settling for it. Thank you
for the twenty-four hours in each day that you allow me to serve and
glorify you, to experience grace and strength in Jesus. May my many
hats not become many identities. Grant me maturity in Christ and
clarity in mission. I ask that you protect me from serving in my own
strength, with my own energy. Holy Spirit, energize your servant
and your people. Thank you that I am not sufficient in myself to
claim anything as coming from within, but that my sufficiency and
strength are from you – by your Spirit alone. Please, keep giving life.
(Ps. 86:11; 2 Cor. 3:4-6)

2

Making Tents and Preaching the Gospel

A Vocational Life

… The Lord commanded that those who proclaim the
gospel should get their living by the gospel. But I have
made no use of any of these rights, nor am I writing
these things to secure any such provision. For I would
rather die than have anyone deprive me of my ground
for boasting.
—1 Corinthians 9:14-15

How does the Lord typically provide for the needs of those He
calls into full-time ministry? The apostle Paul directly answers
this question: "The Lord commanded that those who proclaim
the gospel should get their living by the gospel" (1 Cor. 9:14).
Ministers and their families are generally supported by their
work in the ministry.

The principle is this:

Those who preach the freedom of the gospel should live
with financial freedom in their assigned sphere of influence
(within reason and where it is possible).

While local churches have different capacities from which to support their pastor(s), it is an altogether too common reality that many pastors are barely able to make ends meet, even when they live modestly within the community to which they have been called. Sometimes this is a result of a church's limited resources, other times it may be the result of untimely healthcare needs or the regional housing market. Unfortunately, it can also result from a lack of financial management on the part of the minister. However, there are also many churches that are zealous to give generously to missions, spiritual programs, or to their facility, yet they may be simultaneously stingy when it comes to caring for those who shepherd the flock. This ought not to be as the elders of a local church simply must be aware of the measure of freedom or financial burden experienced in the life of their minister(s) and families.

That said, the point of consideration for us is that – immediately after Paul declares that the local church ought to provide "the living" of those who sow the seed of the gospel among them – he then releases himself from exercising that right. *"But I have made no use of any of these rights, nor am I writing these things to secure any such provision"* (1 Cor. 9:15). Paul did not "make his living" by his work in the gospel. Rather, according to Acts 18:3, he made his living through the work of his hands.

He made tents as he preached the gospel. He preached the gospel as he made tents. Paul was proud of this duality and we can only assume that he made tents with the zeal with which he preached Jesus. He certainly spoke about it with zeal.

> For I would rather die than have anyone deprive me of my ground for boasting. For if I preach the gospel, that gives me no ground for boasting. For necessity is laid upon me. Woe to me if I do not preach the gospel! For if I do this of my

own will, I have a reward, but if not of my own will, I am still entrusted with a stewardship. What then is my reward? That in my preaching I may present the gospel free of charge, so as not to make full use of my right in the gospel (1 Cor. 9:15-18).

Do you sense the tone? Paul did not relinquish this right resignedly. No one made him do it. He boasted of it as a choice that he gladly made. It was his joy to entrust himself to God's provision through a trade he had mastered in tandem with his apostolic calling which remained his priority. Paul was bold and confident about how it all fit together. This was no side-hustle that he tried to keep hidden. No. He testifies that he would rather lose his life than lose his ground of boasting that he chose this route as the most strategic model of life by which he would fulfill his calling. Paul's tentmaking occupation is in no way presented as a distraction or detraction from his vocational ministry.

VOCATIONAL MINISTRY: A SUMMONS

The word vocation derives from the Latin, *vocatio*, which means "a call." It is a summons. An invitation. This is not a ministry semantic. It fits the description of an athlete who gets "called up", or of a teacher or business leader who is offered the job. A call, in the form of an offer, is extended and accepted. This is what makes for a vocation.

Vocational ministry is unique, however, in that the call, or offer, does not come from some hiring manager or the human resources department. It is believed to be a summons from God Himself. In order to discern this calling as being from God, the church historic has clarified that both an internal and external call must be present. Both are necessary.

Internal Calling

The internal call is just that. It is felt and responded to within the heart of a believer who senses a compelling call by the Spirit of God. A call to go, or to serve, or to preach and make disciples. The Scriptures give ample examples of this internal experience among the prophets and preachers of the Old and New Testaments. Perhaps the most obvious example is the call of Isaiah.

> And I heard the voice of the Lord saying, "Whom shall I send, and who will go for us?" Then I said, "Here I am! Send me." And he said, "Go…" (Isa. 6:8-9).

Isaiah heard the voice of the Lord calling out for an ambassador, and his internal desires burgeoned within. With the zeal of a child he responded, "pick me, pick me!" We know that, in accordance with the design of his calling, Isaiah's internal compulsion did not receive an external manifestation or "offer" from the visible church of his day. He did not gain the "manifest approbation of the saints" because of the obvious alignment of his gifting and fitness for the role. Expectantly, the rebellious people of God did not desire to hear the prophetic voice in the wind. Nonetheless, Isaiah sets a model for us of what an internal call looks like, sounds like, and can feel like. It is a holy burden to say yes to the Spirit of God who alone can orient our hearts to the things of God.

I experienced my own internal call when I was in high school. I sensed without a doubt that the Lord had called me to serve in His church within His kingdom on earth. I assumed it was a call to preach and teach the gospel from the Word of God, likely in some traditional role in the local church. However, I would not know this apart from an eventual external call, which thankfully came from a small rural church in East Tennessee. I was twenty-three years old and had completed the requisite theological preparation, yet I had little experience to justify their hopes. In His providence, God orchestrated their affirmation and their provision of an outlet for my calling.

External Calling

You probably know this next bit. But internal desires are not enough. Our desires can be deceptive (Jer. 17:9), even if they are good desires, such as to serve God vocationally. We can easily misinterpret what we feel. One cannot just yearn to serve God and then be self-ordained into a strategic, public ministry. Rather, an actual summons or external calling must be provided through the visible church in an assigned sphere of influence that has been ordered by God.

Ideally, this external calling comes with an obvious "fit" with one's desires, gifts and preparation. It is a moment of confirmation. Think of the experience of young Timothy, the disciple of Paul. From childhood, Timothy had a sincere faith that did not go unnoticed. According to Acts 16:2, he was well-spoken of "by the brothers" in his hometown. Timothy visibly evidenced gifts given to him by God for the service of the people of God. Even more, the leaders in the church at Derbe and Lystra were keen on his maturity. Assumedly, Timothy had internal desires to serve God as well, as his presence and investment in the local church had been impactful in spite of his youth. And yet, Timothy did not have authority to autonomously "follow his feelings" into a self-assigned role in the early church. That is not the way it works. Rather, the affirmation of his calling came through a process that was greater than his desires. When the Apostle Paul came through the region, we read in Acts 16 that he desired and selected Timothy to accompany him.

Timothy was chosen to serve as the First Apostolic Intern. He apprenticed with Paul. He tested his gifts. He made progress in handling the Scriptures. He learned to "share in suffering for the gospel by the power of God, who saved us and called us to a holy calling" (2 Tim. 1:8-9; Acts 16:1-5). And then it happened. At some point, a formal, visible, external call came. Timothy was set apart to serve as a pastor. "For this reason I remind you to fan into flame the gift of God, which is in you through the laying on of my hands" (2 Tim. 1:6). As Paul was nearing the end of his own vocational life, he found it worthy to remind his former intern to look to the past evidences of his own internal and external calling. This is something we must all do.

Calling Matters

It is necessary for us to emphatically ground the discussion that follows with an understanding of calling. This is a foundational reality for all ministers of the gospel, especially those who are called to a bi-vocational life. The reality presented to us in the Word of God, which we must believe, is that:

God gifts those He calls,
  And He calls those He has gifted.
He summons those He sends,
  And He orders their provision and placement.

Do you believe this? It has become apparent to me that many bi-vocational ministers wrestle deeply with their internal and external call. This makes sense. It is difficult to boast in a singular, clear, life calling from God, when our life feels compartmentalized with diverse roles or tasks, some sacred and others more secular; some clearly missional, some mundane. It becomes easy to wonder, "Did I misinterpret my desires when I surrendered to this path? Shouldn't a full-time assignment from God have shown up by now?" For those who feel burdened within a bi-vocational life, it is easy to think: "This was not the plan." But who is to say that it isn't? It was Paul's plan. More than that, it was his boast.

Bi-vocationalism is hard. And yet, if we would allow our feelings to conform to what we see in the Scriptures, then we must lean into the simplicity of this paradigm, more than the complexity of it. We must be willing to boast in it, even when we find ourselves burdened by it. *It is a divine calling, orchestrated by God.*

If you are a bi-vocational minister, sometimes you may feel that your internal calling "got me into this mess." That is not true. You were called into this mess just the same as Isaiah was called into a different mess; or Joseph or Daniel, or Ezra for that matter. You were called and summoned by the Spirit of God to fulfill the plan of God – if you were called at all, in the truest sense. Our Triune God, who alone is perfectly wise, has set you apart that you might serve Him in an assigned and defined role in His redemption of this mess.

Over the last twenty years, I have oft needed to look back and recall the force of my internal calling that propelled me on a journey. The journey providentially included God's provision of an affirming external call. When I feel insufficient "for these things" – for the highs and lows of ecclesiastical and ambassadorial life – I have needed to remember that God put internal desires within me decades before this moment or that moment. This has been true during every stage and placement of ministry. When I was a young husband and father serving as a solo pastor in a small rural church, I desperately needed to be held by a spiritual sense of calling. In my inexperience and fear, I often wondered how God would hold all things together when I was falling apart. Or, years later when navigating the frenetic life of a church planter in the secular and depressed Northeast, I needed to trust that God had called my family to this and that He would provide (even when it felt like we were adding more mouths to feed in our home than He was adding to our core group).

In and throughout every assignment, every pastor needs to trust in the sovereign calling of God, anticipating that He will prove his calling time and again, and often when it is most needed.

If you are in vocational ministry in any capacity, look for brothers whom you labor beside or who serve Christ in a ministry that overlaps your life. Remind them of their calling! Or, if you are a lay-person in the local church who has seen evidence of the calling of God in the life of those who shepherd you – remind them of their calling! The Lord provides for those whom He calls. Bring reminders during times of rest and encouragement as well as during times of duress and burden. We ought to remind one another of our calling, just as Paul reminded Timothy. It is necessary for a vocational life that finishes well. To be redundantly clear: this is true for every minister of the gospel, and it is all the more important for those to whom God has given a bi-vocational assignment.

To my surprise, the Lord has used the complexity of bi-vocationalism to confirm His calling on my life in ways that surpass what I had previously experienced when serving within a traditional model of pastoral ministry. In my younger years as a solo pastor and church planter, I was graciously and regularly affirmed in my calling by those around me. Many older and more mature saints encouraged me, reminding me of the role I was called to fulfill. They held me up in prayer and gave confidence in my preaching, teaching and pastoral leadership. I struggled still, thinking that much of their encouragement came because I was vigilant to fulfill the duties of my position. Pastors pastor. Preachers preach. I was hired to do a job and I was doing it.

Certainly, it was more than that. I have always known that. Ever since I was a young man, I have sensed a call to ministry that came with desires fueled by the Word and Spirit of God. It was never just a job. But once I was in it *as a job,* I slowly began to struggle to feel my calling. Over the years I have found myself privately hoping that my early years' experience in full-time ministry was an exception to the rule, and that most full-time pastors did not wrestle with their calling the way I had. But I did.

And then, something radical changed. I felt called again.

I sensed by the Word and Spirit of God that I was called to do something that I would never want to do or try to do if I was not called to it. Something that I would not have the capacity to do if I was not gifted for it. Something that I would never be able to fulfill if God had not equipped me for it. Bi-vocational ministry has convinced me, again, that being in ministry is only a result of the calling, equipping and sending of God. Calling matters.

And for all those whom God calls, He will provide. To that we now turn.

Four Models of Support

For all those whom God calls, He will provide. There are four models of material and financial provision described in the Scriptures for those who live a life of vocational ministry.

Vocational ministry can be *church-supported* (provided for by the tithes/offerings of the local church to which one has been called), *"tentmaking" supported* (provided for through work in a different skill, trade or job – whether secular or sacred), *missions-supported* (provided for by the gifts of people/churches <u>other than</u> those being served), and *multi-vocationally supported* (provided for through one or more jobs in addition to support from the church being served). Each of these models position a vocational minister to serve God strategically in a full-time capacity.

Church-Supported Vocational Ministry

Generally, when Christians speak of "full-time ministry" they mean fully church-supported. In his first letter to the church at

Corinth the apostle Paul reiterates a command "from the Lord Himself" that the local church provide the necessary material support for those who sow and teach the gospel among them. Paul grounds his argument in common experience as well as the Law of Moses.

> Who serves as a soldier at his own expense? Who plants a vineyard without eating any of its fruit? Or who tends a flock without getting some of the milk? Do I say these things on human authority? Does not the Law say the same? For it is written in the Law of Moses, "You shall not muzzle an ox when it treads out the grain." Is it for oxen that God is concerned? Does he not certainly speak for our sake? It was written for our sake, because the plowman should plow in hope and the thresher thresh in hope of sharing in the crop. If we have sown spiritual things among you, is it too much if we reap material things from you? (1 Cor. 9:7-11, referencing Deut. 25:4)

Notice, the repetition of "in hope" in v.10. The plowman plows in hope. The thresher threshes in hope. What is the implication? Those who preach the freedom of the gospel do so in hope that they also might live in financial freedom through their vocational ministry.

And yet, presumedly, this was not a shared expectation or hope among the church at Corinth. Paul soberly asks: "Is it too much if we reap material things from you?" Apparently, it was too much for some in Corinth. They were too stingy to satisfy the material hopes of those who preached the hope of the gospel among them. This comes as no surprise to most who labor in vocational ministry. Hard-working and lazy pastors (may it not be) alike have had to endure jokes about working one day a week. Even though the apostle Paul asks "is it too much," many church budget meetings awkwardly have included commentary from members who convey that the pastor's below-inflation salary increase "is too much." But to Paul, it is not too much. It is required.

This expectation is not exclusive to the New Testament. In the Old Testament, the pattern had been set. The Levitical priesthood was materially supported by the covenant people of God. By design, the Levitical priests had "no portion or inheritance with Israel." Thus, the Lord commanded that they "receive their due from the people" – whether a portion of the animal sacrifices or of the grain offerings. Why was this? "For the Lord your God has chosen him out of all your tribes to stand and minister in the name of the Lord…" (Deut. 18:5). Because the priest was vocationally called by God, the Lord commanded that his provision come through the people of God. Throughout redemptive history, the Lord has ordered that the material needs of His representatives be provided by the people to whom they minister.

Missions-Supported Vocational Ministry

A second means of provision for vocational ministers is missions-based support. It is not uncommon for a missionary to request support from a sending church, or many sending churches (and individuals), that they might labor to advance the gospel in a different region or among a different people. This can be broadly employed – whether by a foreign missionary or a local campus minister. Missions-supported vocational servants raise support so that they can pour themselves into the people where they have been sent, avoiding a diversion of time or a dilution of focus. Many missionaries must utilize this model as their sole means of sustainability. They may be prohibited from working in the community where they live or they may be unable to "make a living" due to the poverty of their community and the limited resources within the indigenous, local church.

There are biblical examples of believers from one locality in the kingdom of God providing for the needs of an individual or the church in a different region or community in the world. In various of his letters, Paul speaks of the collection that the Gentile church made for the poor within the church in Jerusalem. In Galatia, the church took up a weekly, regular collection (1 Cor. 16:1-4). In 2 Corinthians 8-9, Paul celebrates how "their abundance of joy and their extreme poverty have overflowed in a wealth of generosity" (8:2). They did not give because they held a stockpile of discretionary resources or because it just seemed nice to do. They were motivated by the gospel. As they had come to share in the spiritual blessings of the gospel, they discerned it was right to share and "be of service to them in the material blessings" (Rom. 15:27).

This is the principle that supports all missionary giving. The gospel compels individuals and the church of Jesus to provide material blessing where it is needed among the church on earth. While it is true that the offering of the Gentile church was for the poor within the Jerusalem church and not explicitly for those pastoring or serving in missions or ministry, the principle is the same. God gives generously to His church and He is glorified when that blessing is extended to meet the material needs of Christians in other places.

As Paul writes in 2 Corinthians 9:10-12:

He who supplies seed to the sower and bread for food will supply and multiply your seed for sowing and increase the harvest of your righteousness. You will be enriched in every way to be generous in every way, which through us will produce thanksgiving to God. For the ministry of this service is not only supplying the needs of the saints but is also overflowing in many thanksgivings to God.

It is of note that Paul's own life evidenced this provision by God. To the newly planted church at Rome, he commended his servant and friend, Phoebe, requesting that they offer her assistance as she may have need. He justified his reasoning: because "she has been a patron of many and of myself as well" (Rom. 16:1-2). In some way and for some season of time, Phoebe's generosity supplied Paul's needs. This was in addition to his tentmaking trade, and it rightfully "overflowed in many thanksgivings to God."

"Tentmaking" Vocational Ministry

A third means of divine provision for vocational ministry is through "tentmaking." As has been repeatedly referenced, this model comes to us through the writing and life of the apostle Paul, emphasizing that not all vocational ministers or missionaries have their material needs met by the church they serve or by the church(es) that support them. The apostle Paul gave up his right to be supported by the churches he planted, leaning into God's provision for his life by other means. According to Acts 18:1-4, Paul was a tentmaker. When he arrived in Corinth,

> He found a Jew named Aquila, a native of Pontus, recently come from Italy with his wife Priscilla, because Claudius had commanded all the Jews to leave Rome. And he went to see them, and because he was of the same trade he stayed with them and worked, for they were tentmakers by trade. And he reasoned in the synagogue every Sabbath, and tried to persuade Jews and Greeks.

Paul worked a trade, making tents with his hands. He was a small-business owner, effectively implementing his trade in the various cities where he was sent by God. It is wise for us to imagine that his life included all of the necessary components of a sole proprietorship or small business. In addition to sourcing materials and supplies, he was responsible (in some way) for manufacturing, marketing and sales. Paul was a businessman and an apostle. Generally, he worked a solid week with his hands, and he reasoned in the synagogue every Sabbath. Sometimes he taught more frequently than that. Take his tenure in Athens, for example. We must recognize that his time in the marketplace (daily, see Acts 17:17) perhaps included *both* selling tents and reasoning with the Epicurean and Stoic philosophers, or whoever happened to be there. This is the life of a bi-vocational apostle!

Beyond Priscilla and Aquilla, we can assume that he had additional professional colleagues who shared in his trade. It is reasonable to expect that he had choice vendors and suppliers. How perplexing his relationships must have been as he worked his trade in every marketplace, while being known as a man who was lighting the synagogue on fire.

Simply put, Paul lived off of the resources provided by God through a trade other than church planting or pastoral ministry. And yet, no part of the biblical testimony hints to us that Paul was a part-time apostle because of his "other" job. No. He was fully surrendered to his vocational calling, and he was fully provided for by God through tentmaking (and, at times, patrons like Phoebe).

Bi-vocationally Supported Vocational Ministry
Finally, we come to bi-vocationalism, which is not explicitly referenced nor expressly commanded in the Scriptures. However, it is not without biblical warrant. Ultimately, bi-vocational ministers find that God meets their material and financial needs through *multiple sources*, all of which are biblically authorized and described above. A bi-vocational servant, thus, makes his living by combining resources from

the local church among whom the seed of the gospel is sown, as well as by employment outside of the church (which can come in many forms), and perhaps even by additional missionary-support by Phoebe-esque patrons. More words are not needed here to describe the merits of this model, as it is the goal in the pages that follow to explore the complexities and opportunities held out for those who may be uniquely called by God into a boldly bi-vocational life.

BI-VOCATIONALISM OR CO-VOCATIONALISM

Of late, "co-vocationalism" has surfaced as a new and improved version of bi-vocationalism. Those who prefer this semantic find that the prefix 'bi' refers to a separation between the two vocations. In their view, it is helpful to use the term co-vocation as it infers oneness and a unity between the vocations.

I understand the reason for this adaptation and clarified semantic. However, for the sake of the pages that follow, I believe everything that might be conveyed by co-vocationalism encapsulates what bi-vocational ministry should be, and can be, according to the Scriptures. Nowhere do we see that the apostle Paul's tentmaking job divided his life, deterred his church planting, or distracted preaching. Not in the least.

In the chapters before you, wherever you read the prefix "bi-" please understand: it does not denote two callings. In the best scenarios, the "other job" is hyper strategic for kingdom advancement, utilizing the gifts and establishing the bi-vocational minister as an ambassador for the kingdom of heaven. Ministers of the gospel who serve in multiple vocations do so as one person, created and redeemed by God with a single gift set that ought be used strategically within multiple sectors, for maximum kingdom impact. It is one, undivided life and calling (Ps. 86:11).

It does not matter if the bi-vocational minister is a delivery driver, a nonprofit leader, a school teacher or a carpenter … it is of glorious kingdom impact if one is called by God to use the same mind, soul and body to strategically engage in multiple assigned spheres of influence under the same calling, within one life! (Let the reader not tire of my references to Paul's conviction in 2 Corinthians 10:13!)

GOD PROVIDES FOR EVERY VOCATIONAL MINISTER

There is one fitting final point to be made. God provides. He always provides. He became flesh to provide salvation. He provides the change of heart required to save those He calls to Himself. He provides us with faith and life when we were incapable and dead in our trespasses and sin. He provides our sufficiency when He calls us into ministry. He provides our gifts with which to serve Him and equips us to do the work of ministry. He provides our time and energy by which we might live out His calling. When we fail to live as we ought, He provides reminders in His Word of His grace and forgiveness for those who repent of self-reliance, fear, pride or negligence with stewarding His gifts. He provides us with an assigned sphere of influence, so we can trust Him to use us. It stands to reason and is evident in Scripture, then, that He will provide for the material and financial needs of those He calls to serve Him!

Do you believe this? When God orchestrates an aligned internal and external calling, He does so having already ordained how He will provide. Take, for example, the prophet Elijah. Elijah was told by God in 1 Kings 17 to inform King Ahab that there would be three long years of drought and famine due to the wickedness and rebellion of His people. This was Elijah's vocational task. To speak for the Lord. He could do this, well enough, just by speaking a few sentences to Ahab. The bigger challenge lay in how Elijah, himself, would survive the drought and famine. Of no surprise, the Lord arranged for the material needs of Elijah to be sustainably met in the most miraculous of ways. He would be fed by ravens, morning and evening, if he trusted the Lord and obeyed.

> So [Elijah] went and did according to the word of the Lord. He went and lived by the brook Cherith that is east of the Jordan. And the ravens brought him bread and meat in the morning, and bread and meat in the evening, and he drank from the brook. (1 Kings 17:5-6)

This is what the Lord does. He calls. He sends. He equips. He provides. His provision may come through His church, through a trade, through benefactors, or through a combination of His resources. Or, it may be miraculous through birds in the air. But make no mistake – the Lord sustains those He summons.

A prayer for the bi-vocational minister, to this end.

Lord my provider,
All things are from you, to you, and through you, to you alone be the glory. This includes my salvation in Jesus, my calling into vocational ministry, my specific assignment in your kingdom, and all the providences and people that surround it. It includes all of my mornings and days and nights. My capacity of mind and of body, as well as all of my material needs being met according to your sovereign determination. Thank you for how you provide for this life in which I get to serve you – give me gratitude for my unique vocational arrangement through which you provide for my family. Please, I pray, keep me always depending even as you continue always providing.
To you alone be the glory, Amen.

Part Two

BI-VOCATIONAL MINISTRY EXPLORED

A bi-vocational life, by definition, includes "another" job. This reality multiplies the obligations, responsibilities, demands and expectations that simultaneously pile up throughout any given week, month or year. These are in addition to the higher responsibilities associated with shepherding in the home. It is understandable that this life is not for everyone, nor is everyone called to it. The looming question is: why would one intentionally pursue a boldly bi-vocational life, rather than enduring it only for as long as may be necessary? What makes it worthy of strategic contextualization? In the remaining chapters that follow, we will explore the glory of this calling and the mindset required, considering the costs and benefits, the risks and the rewards.

3

The Glory

A Diversified Kingdom Investment

But seek the welfare of the city where I have sent you into exile, and pray to the Lord on its behalf, for in its welfare you will find your own.
—Jeremiah 29:7

For the bi-vocational minister, as with any minister of the gospel, motive matters. There are a plethora of motives by which God draws people into ministry. What might motivate one whom the Lord calls to *want* to live out their calling within a bi-vocational framework? There are many personal and contextual reasons. Perhaps a minister was in a flexible or strategic secular career prior to sensing a call to ministry, which merged seamlessly into a single life of ministry in multiple vocations. Or, one may have enjoyed a hobby alongside public ministry, which turned into a part-time additional job that remained both strategic for kingdom impact and complementary to formal ministry. Of course, many pastors are hired into a part-time ministry position that they feel compelled and equipped to fill, even though it requires a secondary source of remuneration. This is understandable, sacrificial and beautiful – for both minister and church alike.

Nevertheless, we need to be clear. A boldly bi-vocational life flows out of a motive that is far greater than simply trying to make more money. For some that may be the catalyzing hope or a necessary reality, but it ought not be the driving motive. We are not talking about a "side hustle." Even though the providence of God may provide generous financial provision through a side job, the calling is higher and holier than the provision provided through it. Bi-vocationalism is glorious because, through it, one is positioned strategically to serve God in multiple sectors of the community, simultaneously. One gets to be the aroma of Christ in places and ways that an exclusively church-employed or church-supported vocational minister is unable.

If we consider it from a stewardship angle – the bi-vocational minister is formally positioned to diversify his investment as an ambassador for the kingdom of Jesus.

Let me give an example. My seventeen-year-old son's construction teacher at a large public high school is the pastor of a local Baptist church. He is gifted by God as a communicator, leader, and instructor. Through his intentional bi-vocational life, he gets to lead and instruct others (as well invest God's presence and grace) in both the world and the church, at the same time.

Surprisingly, I learned he was a pastor only after an awkward conversation at a Parent-Teacher Night. That very afternoon I had sent an email to hundreds of regional pastors inviting them to the *Charles Simeon Trust* Workshop on Biblical Exposition that our church was hosting. Unbeknownst to me, he had received my email. When I introduced myself as "Nate's father" he immediately quipped, "Ahh, you're Jim! I got your email today." Wait, what? When did I email you? He then informed me that he had been quietly and effectively serving as a bi-vocational preaching pastor for some time. Small world, so had I.

This brother preaches and pastors weekly in the local church, and yet, in his secular sphere of influence, he daily engages hundreds of young adults. In fact, he said to me: "I would love to come to the workshop, but, you know… these students need me here." (More on the opportunity cost of the bi-vocational life in Chapter 6.) His students *did* need him there. In this secular job he has served countless unbelieving classmates and friends of my son, many of whom I have not met. He has personally invested in Nate, working on after-school projects while influencing his worldview as a believer inside of a secular space. Consider his influence on so many lives in our community, compounded with every year he continues in this arrangement.

One life. One calling. A diversified kingdom investment. This is the glory of bi-vocationalism.

My own continued bi-vocational saunter as a nonprofit leader and consultant has enabled me to engage individuals that I would otherwise not know. Undeniably and often uncomfortably the nonprofit sector is a melting pot of divergent worldviews and hopes. My "other job" has provided innumerable intersections with diverse community leaders who operate out of conflicting values – such as those imposed by large corporations, the government, or by faith-based organizations (often rooted in a social gospel or various shades of unorthodox progressive theology). All of these individuals need the gospel and need to know who Jesus is and why He came, and I would never know them apart from a bi-vocational model of ministry by which God has *placed me* in their world. This is the glory of bi-vocationalism. I have been given an additional sphere of influence wherein to invest, for the glory of God.

My own experience has proven the unstated hypothesis: *rather than diluting the spiritual gifts of a minister or missionary, bi-vocationalism has diversified and intensified the kingdom investment.* It is not a life that is necessarily derailed by distraction or dividedness. Instead, it is a life that brings extreme clarity, focus and purpose. A bi-vocational life has the capacity to enhance the return on investment (ROI) of a single life, lived with strategic intent. It formally positions a servant of Christ to use their unique, ordained gift set in both sacred and secular spaces, forging simultaneous and complementary social, cultural and communal inroads in the ministry and marketplace.

THE GIFTS AND THE GIVER

All who have been saved by God are gifted by God. This is the declaration of Scripture. We have gifts from the Giver. "Every good and every perfect gift is from above, coming down from the Father of lights" (James 1:17).

In Romans 12:4-8, the Apostle Paul writes:

> For as in one body we have many members, and the members do not all have the same function, so we, though many, are one body in Christ, and individually members one of another. Having gifts that differ according to the grace given to us, let us use them: if prophecy, in proportion to our faith; if service, in our serving; the one who teaches, in his teaching; the one who exhorts, in his exhortation; the one who contributes, in generosity; the one who leads, with zeal; the one who does acts of mercy, with cheerfulness.

Paul is emphatic that each member of the body is needed for the health of the whole body. We have been given sovereignly assigned roles to play within His church, according to our gifting: "Now there are varieties of gifts, but the same Spirit; and there are varieties of service, but the same Lord; and there are varieties of activities, but it is the same God who empowers them all in everyone ... All these are empowered by one and the same Spirit, who apportions to each one individually as he wills" (1 Cor. 12:4-6, 11).

It is beautiful, every time and in every place. God calls, assigns, and variously gifts individuals in the body for the maturing of the whole church.

> And he gave the apostles, the prophets, the evangelists, the shepherds and teachers, to equip the saints for the work of ministry, for building up the body of Christ, until we all attain to the unity of the faith and of the knowledge of the Son of God, to mature manhood to the measure of the stature of the fullness of Christ (Eph. 4:11-13).

But here is the question: Are the variously given gifts *only* for the building up of the church? No. Our gifts are to be used both within the redemptive community of the people of God (the church) as well as for the common good of the city (or neighborhood or corporation) where we have been sent. God designs and distributes every gift for every one of His children for a purpose that is greater than just the church taking care of itself.

GIFTED FOR THE COMMON GOOD

This is precisely what Paul says in 1 Corinthians 12:7: "To each is given the manifestation of the Spirit for the common good." Certainly, it is beautiful when a local church has internal capacity to serve one another holistically, both spiritually and commonly in a myriad of ways. However, what about how the Spirit of God empowers the members of the body of Christ to serve the common good of the city where we live, work and play?

This is important to consider. We are sojourners and exiles – not at home in this world. Citizens in a kingdom that is not of this world. We must understand that the God who has saved us and gifted us has also sent us into the precise times and places of our exile, for His purposes that He alone fully knows – though we can assume it is related to His loving discipline, to His gospel spreading through evangelism, to His people bringing cultural redemption, to God-reflecting glory and worship as we live as unto the Lord, and not men. He positions us in His world with government and commerce and art and culture that needs the influence of His redeemed people. We are called to invest and inject *His* justice, *His* mercy, *His* gospel and *His* glory into the social fabric of the communities where we find ourselves. In other words, He has gifted us to impact the common good of the cities where we have been sent.

This is the essence of the letter that Jeremiah the prophet sent from Jerusalem to the surviving elders, priests, prophets and people during their exile to Babylon. Ultimately, Jeremiah instructed the exiles to live where they were sent, and to seek the common good while they were there.

To quote Jeremiah's letter:

Thus says the Lord of hosts, the God of Israel, to all the exiles whom I have sent into exile from Jerusalem to Babylon: Build houses and live in them; plant gardens and eat their produce. Take wives and have sons and daughters; take wives for your sons, and give your daughters in marriage, that they may bear sons and daughters; multiply there, and do not decrease. But seek the welfare of the city where I have sent you into exile, and pray to the Lord on its behalf, for in its welfare you will find your welfare (Jer. 29:4-7).

If this mindset is needed for individual disciples and family units among the covenant people of God – who quite obviously do not fit in a world that is not their home, with cultures and systems that are foreign to the righteousness and redemptive design of God – then it is all the more needed for those who would live within a boldly bi-vocational framework. By the very construct of our lives, we are strategically positioned to seek the welfare of the city where we live, even as we employ our same unique gifts in the church, wherever we have been assigned. We are diversifying our kingdom investment and enhancing the redemptive return for the glory of God.

SHEPHERDS OUT IN THE FIELD

Consider the vast need for wise, righteous, humble Christ-representing leaders within the corporations, organizations, or civil governments of our times – of your city. Across all regions and cultures, does God not purposefully insert His servants into secular spaces for His sovereign purposes? Individuals spend hundreds of hours together each month in boardrooms, on manufacturing floors, on conference calls, or in classrooms. In His wisdom, God positions those whom He has saved to serve the common good and welfare of individuals collected in those places. He orchestrates relationships among the lost and found.

Many who are ignorant of the Word of God, the justice and mercy of God, or the kingdom of Jesus get to be exposed through believers who function as CEOs, salespersons, librarians or lunch ladies. In this regard, every disciple has a vocational call to ministry. Whether one serves within the church as a layleader, elder, teacher or regular member – all disciples of Jesus must seek to make disciples within our vocational sphere of influence. This is all the more descriptive of the divinely orchestrated reality of a tentmaker or bi-vocational minister. A bi-vocational minister is strategically positioned and released by God to represent Christ in the mission field outside of the church, even as he serves as an under-shepherd of Christ within the church. At the same time.

GIFTS THAT FIT

When I took my initial cautious, yet compelled, steps toward a tentmaking (and then bi-vocational) model, I was skeptical that I would find a job that fit. Up to that point, my journey had included only graduate theological studies or church leadership – hardly a path of preparation that would impress a secular employer. I figured the best that I could hope for would be a Christian business owner who might charitably offer me employment, but I was doubtful that a typical corporate hiring manager would place my resume on the top of any pile.

As things progressed, I surprisingly discovered the transferable nature of my previous experience in vocational ministry. I should not have been surprised. The world outside of the church needs the wisdom of God that most naturally flows from the lives of humbled sinners who submit to the Law of God, even as they rest in the unearned mercy they have received from God. In the nonprofit sector where my journey began, there was visible need for skilled communicators, visionaries, collaborators, conflict-arbiters, and encouragers – mercifully strong leaders who could navigate relationships with diverse stakeholders who operated with various value systems and who were seeking different ends. I was no longer in the church, but I found myself immediately using the same gifts from God that

I had been more accustomed to using within the church. It was equally complex, and it was invigorating.

Though I was in a different enterprise, I did not encounter any relationships, situations, leadership decisions or processes that were completely foreign. None. People were still people, made in the image of God living in a world made by God, and they were broken by sin. Pride was still pride. Fear was still fear. Conflict was still in need of resolution. Hope was still longed for, and the purpose of life and the point of today was still a topic of discussion. Every situation required prayer. Every unbecoming joke needed a wise response. Every relationship demanded wisdom, especially with those who had no fear of God. Every management decision required integrity according to God's standard of righteousness, along with a redeemed perspective and purpose as people failed and needed grace. Every day afforded innumerable moments to repent and believe. It was still ministry, just outside of the church. I was in a place in need of a minister who would bring an interpretation and influence according to the sufficient and applicable Word of God.

Honestly, I was revitalized by how much I fit in to that new space. Situations of criticism or conflict, which may have oppressed me within the church, were catalytic toward prayer and emboldened dependence on the calling of God to plant me in this mission field. I was refreshed when I realized that no one was extending any special treatment toward me because "he's our pastor." This had always been troublesome for me in the church. If anything, I found myself operating as an outsider looking in, listening and searching for opportunities of relationship, evangelism or discipleship. Some people knew me to be a pastor, but most did not. This was a good thing. I needed them not to interact with me, positionally, as a minister assigned by God, but to know me, experientially, as a dependent follower of Jesus who needed God's mercy and grace.

This was not as hard as I expected, simply for the fact that *through* the assignment in a secular space, I was exposed to new measures of personal insufficiency, temptations of covetousness, lust, self-reliance and pride. I needed the power of the gospel of Jesus in profoundly new ways (more on this in chapter 5 as it deeply changed my applications in preaching). These were all struggles I felt as a pastor, but this was different. And it profoundly enhanced the kingdom investment I was able to make.

Mostly, I realized that I could not just go into autopilot. I was now off-roading outside of the familiar ruts I had grown accustomed to traveling inside of the church. This new mission field demanded a new, daily focus and intensity. It required a diversified investment of all of my resources into new enterprises, systems and relationships – all of which were too big for me. I prayed fervently and differently. I was forced to lead people creatively. I began to listen more acutely. I presumed less and observed more intently. I felt a renewed call to serve Jesus with a measure of bravery, wisdom, integrity, awareness of the Law of God and repentance at my failures *because I kept failing* in this new arena that was outside of the comfortable "safety" of the local church. I was called daily to enter the world with a redemptive countenance, fearlessly. It was unmistakably clear that through tentmaking (and then bi-vocationalism) I had been positioned by the God of perfect providence to mature as His child. I was made to desperately rely on His empowerment to use the same gifts in totally new and extremely intentional ways.

I am not alone. There are many tentmaking and bi-vocational servants who deploy their unique gifts from God in diversified ways within and without the church. I met my friend Graham Jones at a Simeon Trust workshop in Texas in 2019. Graham serves as an Associate Pastor at a church plant outside of Dallas, prioritizing music and worship leadership amidst a myriad of pastoral duties. Simultaneously, Graham is a professional musician (one of my favorite artists, I might add). In his bi-vocational arrangement, each Fall Graham has been afforded the freedom to step outside of the boundaries of his local church to tour his music across the country – investing his talents and gifts beyond the local church. This is an understandable alignment of how his gifts are used inside and outside of the church – and might be compared to a pastor who also serves as a seminary professor, counselor, or writer. But there is more. For an extended season Graham was able to share the redeeming gift of music in nursing homes around the Dallas–Fort Worth metroplex. He shared the hope of the gospel through music in a challenging realm that is not sexy, easy, or celebrated. Graham is one of many quiet, unsung bi-vocational servants whom I intersected following my own vocational shift. There are examples upon examples of sacrificial and strategic servants who are daily provided for by God through a single gift set, diversely invested in multiple places, simultaneously.

Indeed, to live a boldly bi-vocational life is to stand with one foot in the systems and sectors of this world, investing wisdom, art, justice, mercy and redemptive hope for the common good, even as the other foot is securely planted in the local church, where we serve the redeemed people of God and we are served by people whose hope and life are tethered to Christ. We each do this uniquely, specifically created and redeemed in the image of God, that we might invest our gifts, personalities, minds and resources in diversified places as we are assigned by God. This is the glory of bi-vocationalism.

A prayer for the bi-vocational minister, to this end:

O Lord from whom every perfect gift is given,
If I have been assigned HERE, and if you have called me
HERE – release your empowered gifts HERE so that others
might know of your glory, goodness and kindness revealed in
Christ. Help me to seek the common good and welfare of your
redeemed people and your world in need of your redemption
– as I live out the gospel where you have placed me. As you
see fit, diversify the use of my gifts, making them effective and
efficient for the advancement of your kingdom in multiple
spheres of influence, simultaneously. In whatever roles I play,
would you receive the glory as the fame of Jesus increases, and
I decrease. Amen.
(2 Cor. 10:13; Jer. 29:7)

4

The Mindset

Plundering the Egyptians

So you shall plunder the Egyptians...
Thus they plundered the Egyptians.
—Exodus 3:22; 12:36

I still remembered the first time it came out of my mouth.

"We are plundering the Egyptians, here."

In my tentmaking role leading a housing nonprofit, I had just returned from a meeting with the executive leadership of a major corporation whose social responsibility goals included the prioritization of adequate housing for low-income families. While their corporate values could in no way be called biblical or holy, this entity zealously cared for basic human needs, dominantly shelter. The proposal we put forward was embraced and a significant six-figure investment was made in our mission. Understand, they were a publicly traded secular corporation, and we were a faith-based construction organization that hosted mission-trip experiences wherein youth received workforce development training even as they were discipled to follow Jesus. To be clear, they were not directly investing in Christian discipleship. This would be out of conformity to their policies and priorities for social responsibility. Rather, they were investing in materials and supplies for homes that would be repaired free of charge to low-income families. After learning of their investment, I called a Board member: "We are plundering the Egyptians, here."

Literally, we were using the wealth of a secular, earthly corporation to support the mission of God. This major corporation knowingly and repeatedly committed resources to fund home repair projects that would be completed by youth from area churches, who were living out the gospel while learning construction skills – all under the oversight of discipleship-minded licensed contractors and employees who were modelling the humility of Jesus. It was a creative plunder that supported the mission of the church and by which God provided for my family, so that I might freely volunteer as a pastor in the local church.

This is how we should view bi-vocational or tentmaking ministry whenever a minister of the gospel is positioned within a secular corporation or civil vocation. It is modern-day plunder. God, who owns everything, provides for His servants through resources that, on the surface, *appear* to be owned by, managed by, or originating from the kingdom of this world. But they are not. They belong to the Lord. He has everything at His disposal, to be utilized for His sovereign purposes.

> For from him and through him and to him are all things.
> To him be glory forever. Amen (Rom. 11:36).

This is how God works and it is always for His glory, forever. Consider the experience of the exiles who, after Persia ousted Babylon their oppressor, were authorized to return to Jerusalem to rebuild the temple, but not without being "granted" the resources of Persia for the task (Ezra 3). God had turned the heart of the Persian King, Cyrus, whom He had strategically positioned among the nations, to accomplish His ends for the good of His people and the glory of His name.

> So they gave money to the masons and the carpenters, and food, drink, and oil to the Sidonians and the Tyrians to bring cedar trees from Lebanon to the sea, to Joppa, *according to the grant that they had from Cyrus king of Persia.* (Ezra 3.7, emphasis added).

There I was, writing grants to corporate and civil entities whom God had positioned for the glory of His name, the good of His people, and the extension of His mercy. Through it, not only were real construction costs covered, but I was able to serve as an elder and pastor in the local church, such that the church was not financially burdened to provide material support for my family. This, then, indirectly expanded the capacity of the congregation to invest in other avenues of missions and ministry. It is plunder.

My life and the local church where I served were not the lone beneficiaries. With these same resources I was privileged to hire, deploy, and mature alongside multiple gifted and honest full-time employees who facilitated our construction mission even as they were active laypersons, servants and teachers in their local church. Their family's material needs were also met through this plunder!

A BIBLICAL FRAMEWORK OF PLUNDER

Throughout the Bible, the people of God repeatedly experience the plundering provision of God. The phrase "plunder the Egyptians" derives from Exodus 3:20-22. The Lord gives

Moses final instructions to lead the Israelites out of Egypt. They were His nation, and He had seen their affliction. The Lord told Moses that the king of Egypt would neither listen nor comply with the Lord's demand. Nor would he care of his noncompliance. Pharaoh could not care less about the worship of God, the redemption of God, the people of God or the purposes of God. He was one of many kings of the nations who raged against the Lord, even as the Lord sits in the heavens and laughs (Ps. 2:1-3). Consider the word of the Lord to Moses before anything went down:

> I will stretch out my hand and strike Egypt with all the wonders that I will do in it; after that he will let you go. And I will give this people favor in the sight of the Egyptians; and when you go, you shall not go empty, but each woman shall ask of her neighbor, and any woman who lives in her house, for silver and gold jewelry, and for clothing. You shall put them on your sons and on your daughters. *So you shall plunder the Egyptians.*" (Exod. 3:20-22, emphasis added.)

God provided for His people through a voluntary plunder. Those who rejected God released their possessions for the use of God in caring for His people!

This "plunderous" provision by God shows up throughout the history of Israel. Consider the remnant of people that navigated the wilderness and arrived safely in the Promised Land. Moses commanded them in Deuteronomy 6.4-12:

> Hear, O Israel: The Lord our God, the Lord is one. You shall love the Lord your God with all your heart and with all your soul and with all your might. And these words that I command you today shall be on your heart. You shall teach them diligently to your children, and shall talk of them when

you sit in your house, and when you walk by the way, and when you lie down, and when you rise.

Yes, but where did said "houses" come from? God's wandering people did not build them. They did not sign a lease to rent them. They were plundered, and fully furnished at that.

> And when the Lord your God brings you into the land that he swore to your fathers, to Abraham, to Isaac, and to Jacob, to give you—with great and good cities that you did not build, and houses full of all good things that you did not fill, and cisterns that you did not dig, and vineyards and olive trees that you did not plant—and when you eat and are full, then take care lest you forget the Lord, who brought you out of the land of Egypt, out of the house of slavery. [13] It is the Lord your God you shall fear.

The God of plunder provides for His people! The pattern just keeps repeating itself.

Recall 1 Samuel 17, when young David arrived at the valley of Elah with a lunch for his brothers who were stationed on the front lines against the Philistines. Goliath of Gath arrogantly taunted the army of God, demanding a challenger. Ironically, the assumed challenger, who had been unanimously chosen by the people, was nowhere to be found. King Saul cowardly watched from a distance, afraid because slavery was on the line.

> [But] David heard him (1 Sam. 17:23).

How did it all unfold from that moment? We know that there was a bold declaration by David that "the battle belongs to the Lord." There was bickering immaturity among his brothers, an awkward fitting for armor that did not fit, and finally there was a single stone that forever silenced the taunting giant. But beyond that – what was the next experiential reality for the paralyzed Israelite soldiers and for the corporate people of God? PLUNDER.

This is often missed in the story, partly because of the length of the chapter but mostly because of the church's moralistic fixation on David. A little biblical typology can go a long way to help us not miss the point. And we must not miss the point! 1 Samuel 17:53 declares that the next actionable experience of the people of God was to plunder the camp of the Philistines because the Anointed of God had defeated the enemy of God! This is a gospel reality that results in plunder! Because of the victory of the one man whom God would raise up to stand in the gap – His Anointed King – the possessions and riches and weapons of the kingdom of this world (that was opposed to God) became the possessions and riches and weapons of the people in the kingdom that belonged to God. This is the plunder that God provides, and it sounds altogether anticipatory of what John heard in heaven: "The kingdom of the world has become the kingdom of our Lord and of his Christ, and he shall reign forever and ever" (Rev. 11:15).

TENTMAKING AND BI-VOCATIONAL MINISTRY AS PLUNDERING

The New Testament does not speak as often or as tangibly about plunder. This is reasonable, because the New Testament records the expansion of the kingdom of God from a single nation to a church among all nations. We do not expect the church to literally or physically plunder geopolitical spaces. However, it is in the New Testament where we learn that *right now* the kingdom of God is plundering Satan as the Spirit of God converts individual hearts and sets sinners free from sin and death, and as the church on earth experiences the multiplication of those whom God is saving and sanctifying.

This is what Jesus declares in Matthew 12:25-30. Jesus had just healed a demon-oppressed man who was blind and mute, and in response the Pharisees comforted one another that His power to heal derived from His collusion with Beelzebul, the prince of demons. They were quite wrong.

> Knowing their thoughts, [Jesus] said to them, 'Every kingdom divided against itself is laid waste... And if Satan casts out Satan, he is divided against himself. How then will his kingdom stand?'

Satan is not stupid. Satan had nothing to do with this. In fact, Satan could not stop this if he tried, for this act of healing was God's work of PLUNDER through the power of His Anointed. Jesus continued:

> But if it is by the Spirit of God that I cast out demons, then the kingdom of God has come upon you. Or how can someone enter a strong man's house and plunder his goods, unless he first binds the strong man? Then indeed he may plunder his house. Whoever is not with me is against me, and whoever does not gather with me scatters.

Make no mistake, in every place where the church on earth is faithfully present – planting the seed of the gospel and gathering the harvest from God – there is plunder. This does not mean that we get to take the lands or houses or jewelry of those whom God conquers and converts. Rather, it means that in every pulpit where the Word of God is boldly proclaimed, there is plunder. Every time any mouth confesses the name of Jesus, there is plunder. Wherever servants of God are strategically positioned within the kingdoms of this world – amidst corporations, organizations, structures, governments or systems – there is plunder.

This is happening all the time in the rhythms of our lives as we sojourn in this world within our assigned spheres of influence. For example, one of my hobbies for the last fifteen years has been to serve as a soccer coach for my children's club soccer teams. Having played college soccer, as did my wife, it has always been an area of natural investment. Eventually it matriculated into a tiny, part-time vocation, basically covering the expense for our family. Through it I have been afforded hours and weeks and years to invest in the lives of little girls who have become young ladies. While many of the girls moved on to play college soccer, like my daughters, most did not. But this is just fine because that was never the point.

Through coaching, I have experienced the most obvious plunder from God. While I am by no means as faithful or gifted as an evangelist or shepherd as I ought to be, through this small athletic vocation, God ordained for "coach Jim" to serve as "pastor Jim" out in the community. A few of the girls now call me that. Most wouldn't want to. Some wouldn't know what it means.

And yet, God has orchestrated many moments of shepherding. He has positioned me to be present during intense times of need wherein I was able to share the gospel: the death of siblings, the death of classmates, the darkness of depression and anxiety, the divorce of parents, the guilt of sin and sexual immorality, the struggles with sexual identity and gender. I have been able to speak about the design of God and the forgiveness of God from the Word of God. I have been asked to "preach a devotion" (whatever that means) prior to big games, or before season-ending banquets.

Understand, every element of what I have been asked to do in relation to youth sports is NOT a ministry within the church or established by the church. I know some churches do this, but that is a different reality altogether. What I am emphatic about is this: the church where I serve did not create the soccer club and it does not financially support it as a mission outlet. It does not manage the fields or any part of the enterprise. Rather, the church releases me into a space "out in the world" that (on the surface) is governed by citizens of the world, through which I interact with hundreds of kids every week and by which my family is minimally supported. This is plundering! God, in His sovereignty, enables relationally competent image bearers to organize enterprises that the church can use, steward, infiltrate and impact for the glory of God. We do not create these outlets. We use them. We benefit from them. This is plundering.

LEARNING FROM LAITY

Ultimately, every lay Christian who participates in the local church while being vocationally employed within the sectors and enterprises of our world, is positioned by God to plunder the world and advance the redeeming kingdom of Christ in that space. Even more, God provides for their family's material needs through it! It is all plunder, and we must go about it strategically.

Every Christian teacher employed within a government school is a participant within a mandated gathering of children and adults, and is thus positioned to "plunder the Egyptians" by direct or covert approaches to teaching their discipline from a worldview governed by God's Word, as well as in how they relate to students and colleagues. They are financially supported and positioned by a secular institution, wherein they can speak for God into the lives of those brought to them by God.

For some, this may primarily be evidenced through relational influence inside and outside of the classroom, as it is obvious to others that "in your hearts you honor Christ the Lord as holy." As a result, God provides relational opportunities to "make a defense of the hope within you" (1 Pet. 3:15). For others, the plunder is more turbulent, as they collide with school administration or colleagues because they have chosen to publicly refute the falsity of what they are told to teach. Perhaps this is you. As Peter says one verse earlier (1 Pet. 3:14), even if you suffer for righteousness sake, you experience the blessing and fearlessness that comes from God having positioned you right where you are, for His purpose *and* your provision. It is all plunder!

Every corporate executive who seeks to steward their wealth and influence for the glory of God and the good of His kingdom gets to plunder the enemy who is not able to bind the hearts of those who will respond to the gospel, wherever and whenever it is presented. Whenever a Christian businessperson wisely navigates diversity, equity and inclusion (DEI) initiatives with a biblically-nuanced depiction of sexuality, gender or race, they are plundering the kingdom of this world as creational evangelists. Whenever a city council seat is filled by a Christian who faithfully seeks to represent the ethics and design of God for civilians and for civil government (Rom. 13) – there is plunder, even though the authorities of this world may rage in vain (Ps. 2). Have no fear, the sovereign Lord looks down on the threats that the rulers of this world make against his servants. He sees. And He answers the prayers of His disciples who joyously serve Him and speak with boldness wherever they have been placed (Acts 4:23-31).

The church where I serve in Johnson City, Tennessee is blessed to have a congregant who has been vocationally deployed to serve as an executive leadership coach across the world for three decades, while also serving as an elder during many of those years. For this leader, every day in the corporate realm is purposeful and every day is plunder. Not only has his family been provided for by God through his global experience and employment, but his Christian influence has also been expansive across continents! Mark's fingerprints are increasingly found within local corporations as well as among the C-suites of global companies. I can attest that his training of human beings made in the image of God is baked with the design of God according to the Word of God, as well as introducing them to the redeeming nature of God and the ethic of God's kingdom.

Recently, Mark provided data-driven, performance-enhancing coaching to our local church staff. Of course, he customized his content for his audience, translating all things through the lens of the gospel, under the authority of the Word for the good of Christ's church. We are not a corporation and we do not want to be – but we knew we could benefit from his organizational knowledge and experience. As I had expected, the material Mark used with our church staff was the same material he has used across a variety of secular institutions! Mark is continually applying the wisdom of the God to all whom God sets before him.

In his coaching book, *Revealing the Invisible*, Mark writes:

> People are like white light before it enters a prism. Coaching serves as a prism to bring out the talent, helping others to discover what is already within them. Our desire is to draw out [what is there]… C. S. Lewis summarizes it well when he said, 'We are not yet even half-done.' People have amazing capabilities, and often many of our capabilities stay hidden within us. Coaching can help bring out the unique design within others so they can uniquely impact their world.[1]

Mark may as well be quoting Genesis 1:26-27, that we have been uniquely made, male and female, in the image of Trinity

---

1 Mark Hecht, *Revealing the Invisible; Coaching the People You lead to Discover, Learn, and Grow*, (United States: Ignite Press, 2020), p.12.

God. From East Tennessee, Mark is plundering the Egyptians by delivering the wisdom of God to people outside of the church who can only understand one another and pursue a common goal because they have been made in the image of a relational, designing, ordered God. And this provides for his family as they participate in the kingdom of God on earth. This is plunder!

Let the boldly bi-vocational reader understand. If this is true of the laity in the church on earth who are vocationally deployed amidst the kingdoms of this world and who operate with a missionary mindset in the very realms through which God provides their material need, then it must be all the more true for a bi-vocational or tentmaking minister of the gospel who has surrendered to a life of called ministry. When the Lord, the King over all the kingdoms of this world, sovereignly gifts and inserts a pastor who has been trained to understand and communicate His Word into the redemptive economy of His kingdom, we must live with an anticipation of just how glorious God's return on investment will be. He knows the plunder He is gaining!

PLUNDERING IS ALWAYS URGENT

Bi-vocational minister, give yourself to this model, boldly and urgently. It is God's plunder, not merely for your financial provision, but for His mission! It would do us well to return to where we started and observe the intensity and urgency of the plunder that God provided for His people when they left Egypt. In that moment, the people of Israel were not fixating on the plunder to come. Assumedly it was nowhere on their minds. Rather, they were called to fixate on the glory of their saving God, and on the very specific words from Moses about the Passover meal that they were to eat in haste and in obedience. The plunder came on the heels of a moment of communal urgency and focused obedience to the LORD's command. Look at what Exodus 12:11 says, "In this manner you shall eat it: with your belt fastened, your sandals on your feet, and your staff in your hand. And you shall eat it in haste. It is the Lord's Passover."

As they obeyed, it happened. On that horrendous night of judgment, the Lord struck down the firstborn across the land of Egypt, with the tenth and final plague. However, He passed over His people. Picture the Israelite family units huddling together until morning, with parents covering the ears of their children as they endured "the great cry" that resounded throughout Egypt. They waited through it all with sandals on their feet and staffs in their hand. And then – that very night – Moses and Aaron were summoned by Pharaoh. "Get out. Go. You and your people. Go and serve the Lord." It was time to move, urgently. The grieving Egyptians said the same. They urgently sent them out of their scorched land. And so it was that the urgency of the Passover became the urgency of the exodus, and it culminated in an urgent plunder.

> The people of Israel had also done as Moses told them, for they had asked the Egyptians for silver and gold jewelry and for clothing. And the LORD had given the people favor in the sight of the Egyptians, so that they let them have what they asked. Thus they plundered the Egyptians (Exod. 12:35-36).

Urgent plunder, experienced in trust of the God who rescues and provides. This is the story of the people of God from then until now. It is important to finally observe that the material goods of Egypt were not the only plunder. The provision of God was even greater according to Exodus 12:38: "A mixed multitude also went up with them, and very much livestock both flocks and herds." Some of the pagan Egyptians – having been convinced either of the glory of the God of Israel or of the impotence of the gods of Egypt, or both – urgently followed the people from the darkness into the light. It is all plunder!

Plundering is the Lord's way of provision, and it is always an urgent reality. It is not always easy, nor is it always joyous. But it is always urgent.

We must hold this in our minds if we believe that the strong man is bound and that the kingdom of Jesus is currently plundering the kingdoms of this world. If you would be *boldly* bi-vocational, you must work and serve wherever God has placed you with urgency. With urgent obedience. Urgent worship. Urgent work. We must not merely resign ourselves to surviving "two jobs." No. We get up in the morning to experience God's plunder. We ought go to sleep at night with our sandals on our feet and staff in our hand.

A prayer for the bi-vocational minister, to this end:

O Lord, as I serve where you have called, help me to fixate on your glory, your holiness, your mercy and on your promised plunder. Thank you that the strong man is bound and that your Anointed has defeated sin and death and that we can plunder the kingdoms of this world as we follow Him. Help me to trust that you, O Sovereign King, have everything in your hand and that you have predestined all that will be – which includes our participation in your kingdom's advancement and our provision through it. Help me to not merely survive the complexity and busyness of this bi-vocational life, but to enjoy it, urgently, as plunder for your glory and for the good of your kingdom. Amen.
(Acts 4:24-31)

5

The Surprise

The Same Word, The Same Preacher

Therefore, having this ministry by the mercy of God, we do not lose heart. But we have renounced disgraceful, underhanded ways. We refuse to practice cunning or to tamper with God's word, but by the open statement of the truth we would commend ourselves to everyone's conscience in the sight of God.
—2 Corinthians 4:1-2

Bi-vocational ministry can transform the effectiveness of a preacher or teacher of the Word of God. This discovery came as a welcome surprise within months of my transition out of a traditional paradigm of ministry. When I began working another day job, I could never have imagined just how much my preaching as well as pastoral ministry in general would change for the better.

As a teaching pastor, I have always been committed to expository preaching. For more than two decades, it is functionally the only thing I have known that I *must do* –

laboring to preach the finished work of Jesus from every part of the Scriptures. Throughout my vocational transition, I committed that I would not allow this seismic shift to give me any excuse to let my preaching preparation slide. I would do whatever was necessary to keep the ministry of the Word central, which mostly meant earlier mornings and less sleep. Even when I was working full-time as a nonprofit executive, the preaching of the Word remained a higher and holier priority above every other vocational task. While I have never been able to perfectly keep this commitment (daily demands or stupid distractions assault every pastor), God has mercifully compelled me to keep pursing this commitment.

For the bi-vocational minister, there should be no question which aspect of our layered vocational life remains of highest importance. While we work laboriously in a variety of day jobs or roles – and this is a good thing – our trusting that the Word WORKS is the greater good. Our giving ourselves to this task, to the preaching of the gospel from the Scriptures, is paramount. This is the core conviction of an expository preacher. The Word of God always works for God's intended ends, every time it is declared.

> How are they to hear without someone preaching? And how are they to preach unless they are sent? As it is written, "How beautiful are the feet of those who preach the good news!" But they have not all obeyed the gospel. For Isaiah says, "Lord, who has believed what he has heard from us?" *So faith comes from hearing, and hearing through the word of Christ* (Rom. 10:14-17, emphasis added).

> For as the rain and the snow come down from heaven
>   and do not return there but water the earth,
> making it bring forth and sprout,
>   giving seed to the sower and bread to the eater,

so shall my word be that goes out from my mouth;
   it shall not return to me empty,
but it shall accomplish that which I purpose,
   and shall succeed in the thing for which I sent it
(Isa. 55:10-11)

THE WORD WORKS

Expositional preaching simply means that the preacher works to expose, or pull out, what is in the Word of God, fighting against the temptation to insert anything that is not there. Anything. Preachers have no creative license to try and enhance the meaning of a text, lest we deny it in the process. We must believe and remember that we are not originators of content, we are merely translators of what God has declared. The eighteenth-century preacher, Charles Simeon, expressed this conviction well:

> My endeavor is to bring out of Scripture what is there, and not to thrust in what I think might be there. I have a great jealousy on this head: never to speak more or less than I believe to be the mind of the Spirit in the passage I am expounding.

This means that we must labor to handle the Word of God the way that Jesus did. In Luke 24, following His resurrection, Jesus made it clear that every part of the Scriptures were about HIM – from the Law to the historical writings to the Prophets to the Psalms. The suffering, death and resurrection of Jesus are the gravitational center of the Bible! Thus, if we preach the Word faithfully, we will always preach Jesus unapologetically.

For the last twenty years, in an effort to more faithfully handle the Word of God when I preach, I have regularly participated in Workshops on Biblical Exposition hosted by the Charles Simeon Trust. These workshops are gatherings of preaching and teaching pastors from different denominations and contexts who come together to work on our Word work – all believing that the Word of God is inerrant, inspired and sufficient to accomplish all of God's ordained purposes. The workshops are filled with wrestling preachers who push one another to keep making progress in our Word work, collectively fighting against the temptation to get lazy or go into autopilot. As Paul instructed Timothy:

> Practice these things, immerse yourself in them, so that all may see your progress. Keep a close watch on yourself and on the teaching. Persist in this, for by so doing you will save both yourself and your hearers (1 Tim. 4:15-16).

I rehearse all of this, in part, to appeal to every pastor who might be reading, bi-vocational or otherwise. You must labor to make progress in faithfully declaring the good news of Jesus *from the text* you are preaching or teaching or sharing. Believe that the Word works! Give yourself to the task of understanding it before communicating it. Use whatever time you have been afforded. Find a Simeon Trust workshop or any other avenue that will help you make progress.

FAITHFULNESS OVER CREATIVITY

I am abundantly thankful that the calling to preach is about faithfulness not creativity; that the goal of preaching is progress, not perfection; and that the content of our preaching is the Word of God not the words of my mouth or thoughts in my mind. This is glorious news for every imperfect messenger whose sin and insufficiency should easily disqualify us from the task. God is merciful to save us, to sanctify us, and to speak through us! We have no sufficiency in ourselves to claim anything as having come from us. Our sufficiency is only from God who has made us competent to the task (2 Cor. 2:4-5)!

Let the busy bi-vocational preacher boast in the truth that effective preaching is not about human cleverness! This reality is of great comfort to bi-vocational ministers whose bandwidth is likely already stretched thin and who do not have time to be creative, even if they have been blessed with the wit. Thanks be to God that we do not need to find extra hours each week to learn new tricks by which we can be effective when we preach. God mercifully makes us effective as we simply share His Word.

> Therefore, having this ministry by the mercy of God, we do not lose heart. But we have renounced disgraceful, underhanded ways. We refuse to practice cunning or to tamper with God's word, but by the open statement of the truth we would commend ourselves to everyone's conscience in the sight of God (2 Cor. 4:1-2).

In other words, we commend ourselves to God and we position ourselves to be effective only so much as we seek to declare what is in the text. Faithful preaching, not creative preaching, is persuasive preaching. The book of Acts records this time and again, whether the preacher of reference is Peter, Stephen, or Paul. From the whole Scriptures they explained the Law, the Prophets, the Psalms – pointing to the death and resurrection of Jesus – and God made it persuasive (Acts 2:37,41; 4:4; 17:4).

A PERSUASIVE ARRANGEMENT

Here is the point for our consideration. The very paradigm of bi-vocational or tentmaking ministry is an opportunity to believe this and to give ourselves to it, trusting that it is enough. In fact, so long as we labor to understand and communicate the simple meaning of the text, our vocational model helps with our persuasiveness rather than hinders it. It is a providential blessing that the bi-vocational preacher typically has neither the time, the energy, nor the capacity to divulge in excessive creativity or applicational brainstorming. Those who seek to faithfully serve in multiple vocations may necessarily be prevented from keeping up with the latest cultural semantic or nuanced ideological or political realities that might be referenced in their preaching (this is likely true of traditionally vocational pastors). This can be a merciful protection against unhelpful preaching, or worse, from homiletical abuse.

There are simply too many other obligations that press on the time of a bi-vocational or tentmaking pastor. Many bi-vocational pastors have to spend their days delivering packages, leading corporate sales teams, teaching students, or managing a manufacturing floor. Whatever the individual case, this means that the time we *make* to be in the Word is forced to be spent on getting the text right, understanding it within its context, discerning the gospel connection – and preparing to tell it like it is. That is all. And when we do this faithfully as we labor in the world outside of the church, we have profound applicational connections from which to pull as we prepare to apply the point of the text. Thus, rather than diluting the impact of our Word ministry, our vocational construct enhances it!

Consider this. Bi-vocational ministry provides increased firsthand exposure to realities in the world that need the gospel to be applied in ways that are likely not as readily apparent to a non-bi-vocational pastor whose life and leadership are dominantly within the church. Understand what I am not saying. I am not saying that the "ivory tower" is not a good place for a pastor to be, as he labors in his study to understand and then declare the text of God's Word. No! Minister of the gospel – seek to be in your study! Spend time in undistracted, prayerful preparation as you are able, that you might comprehend the meaning of the Word of God before you try and communicate with your audience. You must do this. I bristle when I hear pastors announce that their best sermon preparation is not in their study, but when they are out meeting with others in discipleship, evangelism, or hanging out in their community "third places." As important as those times and spaces are and as they do create intersections of application – they do not replace the need for diligent searching of the Scriptures to understand the meaning for the original hearer, or how the biblical or literary context clarifies the meaning of the text, or how the New Testament applies the text to Christ and His church. A conversation with a friend in a coffee shop about lust or anger cannot replace this, but rather is an expected reality that comes with it.

Here is what I am intimating: when a bi-vocational pastor stands in the pulpit, assuming the text being preached is understood in its context and applied with faithfulness through the gospel of Jesus, that pastor has profoundly benefited from firsthand exposure to the life, systems and culture of the world outside of the church. He stands with one foot in the world and one foot in the study, every day of every week. If God has indeed "determined [our] allotted periods and the boundaries of their [our] places" (Acts 17:26), then the tentmaking or bi-vocationally positioned pastor is stationed by God to both wrestle with and apply the Word of God for two audiences/sectors, simultaneously.

PERCEPTION MATTERS

The non-bi-vocational or tentmaking ministry leader may not easily comprehend what I am saying. That is fair enough. Let me try and explain. Every pastor who preaches or teaches regularly must continually work to understand not only the text they are expositing, but the people to whom they are communicating. It is our calling to frame clear, persuasive arguments and applications from the Scriptures that are personal, cultural and contextual.

Following a sermon, many pastors have experienced someone approaching them, saying: "How did you know? It was like you were talking directly to me." This can be encouraging, unless it is the same person every week. (You know who you are.) The truth is, a pastor usually doesn't know. Both Scripture and experience attest that we cannot fully know what is going on in the hearts, homes, or workplaces of those who hear. We try to know. We try to apply the text, but we cannot fully know all the ways to apply the Word. That is knowledge held by the Holy Spirit alone.

And yet, we *are* able to make many persuasive applicational connections. We *can* presuppose that people in a fallen world wrestle with idolatry that comes in many forms. We *can* apply the law and gospel of God in real ways to people who live in a culture of expressive individualism that comes with destructively fluid definitions of what is good or beautiful or should define our identity. We *can* expose to legalists how they may be strict in their application of the Word of God to others, but how liberal they may be in their application of it to themselves. We *can* and *must* make it plain that people in every generation and culture unwisely and dangerously find new ways to abuse money, relationships and power. Across time, people have struggled because they functionally believe that addictions or relational strife or worldly temptations are impossible and will win in the end. No, they are not impossible, and no, they do not defeat Christ and those who find their refuge in Him. Nothing on earth is more powerful than the resurrection power of Jesus, who, following the interchange with the rich young man, told His disciples: "with man this is impossible, but with God all things are possible" (Matt. 19:26).

We are able to perceive all of those things, generally, to which we can apply the gospel potently. More than that, we can read the headlines on the front page of our local newspaper or in the Wall Street Journal to understand regional and societal cultural issues. We are informed, at some level, of the myriad of realities that people are navigating and we can seek to apply the argument of a particular text as it relates to those issues.

However, for my first decade in ministry, try as I may to understand and apply the gospel, I could not really know what it was like to get up and go to work in a secular institution working for a corporation with ungodly values, even though it was the experience of many in the congregation. I was not able to existentially comprehend what it was like to live in fear of an angry, godless manager, or to struggle with flirtation from an attractive or seducing coworker. I could not fully empathize with the loneliness and the acute temptations suffered by believing exiles who travelled regularly for work, and the challenge it could present for their marriage and family. I understood the nature of pride and self-sufficiency, but I did not know what it was fully like to experience accolades from a big sale (or account) that also came with a huge commission check. I could keep going. All of these things *I tried to understand and speak into* as I preached the gospel from the text I was expounding, but my perception was limited.

Understand, however, that this does not mean that a pastor who serves Christ from within a traditional paradigm of full-time ministry, who may work dominantly in a church building among staff members who have been hired to serve in ministry together and who hold a similar gospel grid and who thus does not receive firsthand exposure to these things, is *unable* to effectively preach the Word and apply the gospel to hearers in these situations. That is not true. We can, by God's Spirit who makes the Word effective, apply His Word in a way that it *works*. Thanks be to God!

But, I had no idea how much tentmaking and bi-vocational ministry would expand my perception of the applicability of the gospel as I began to realize the constancy and heaviness of these realities in the lives of those to whom I preached. I now knew some of these realities in my own life.

THE WEIGHT OF PERCEPTION

I remember keenly the first time I experienced crushing failure in my vocation outside of the church. Following my reception of untimely revenue-impacting news, I was forced to make phone calls to members of the Board of Directors to explain a sudden, pressing organizational challenge. In those moments of rehearsing my failure, I discovered a measure of anger, shame and embarrassment unlike anything I had experienced in the pastorate. While this may have been a result of my immaturity and fear of man, nevertheless it created a radical moment of exposure. Think of George Bailey and his response to the missing bank deposit in *It's a Wonderful Life*. That was me, or so I felt.

I had failed to properly file and receive a grant that the organization had depended upon for many years. It was a significant five-figure annual award that was directly connected to staffing. In losing the revenue source, not only did I risk losing a solid relationship with a funder, I risked losing a solid employee. The loss of this particular employee would mean disaster for the organization's programs and desperation for his wife and children as he would be forced to look for another job. Family security matters, especially having been a church planter on a modest income. I had never known such sudden failure in my vocational and professional life. In an instant, I succumbed to fear, doubt and situational depression. I scared myself.

Wait. Is this what wrestling believers, exiles and sojourners in this world, could possibly feel when they come to worship on a Lord's Day, hearing the Word of God preached? I had no idea. I thought I did. But this was deeper. This meant that when I preached the Bible, it was potentially to people asphyxiated with this much despair, feeling as though they *have been* crushed, not just afflicted; feeling *total* despair, and not just perplexity (to reverse the apostle Paul's confident assertion about our gospel hope in 2 Corinthians 4:8).

That is only the half of it.

I then had to find a way to lead the organization out of a significant financial trial. This is when I discovered how zealously I would work in an effort to fix something that I felt responsibility for messing up. I put everything else aside – sleeping, eating, and family – shameful as it sounds. I made promises to others that I intended to fulfill with my own strength. I sought solutions with my own acumen. I knocked on doors and wrote proposals. I did so in such a way that those who hired me would take notice. I was not only *not* going to lose this employee, I *was* going to raise enough money to hire someone else.

And the worst thing happened. It worked.

A new corporate donor entered the story, and I saw our losses turn into double gains. I celebrated with our staff. I wrote press releases to market the new corporate partner. Once again, I made some phone calls. I called members of the Board of Directors and reported the success, only to be reminded why I was the man for the job and how far the organization had come. I was reminded why "increased revenue" was the dominant variable for a successful year-end evaluation and that it would translate into some form of bonus. I went to bed wondering if the new corporate investment would be in the paper the next morning.

Then it hit me. *Wait. Is this what wrestling believers, exiles and sojourners in this world, could possibly feel when they come to worship on a Lord's Day, hearing the Word of God preached?* Even though I knew it to be possible, I really had no idea how easy and deep is the pull toward self-congratulation and self-sufficiency, and how important was the preaching of the gospel from the Word to confront the prideful, calling them to self-emptying repentance. Every week. Over and over. This meant that when I preached the Bible, it was potentially to people intoxicated with this much pride, who experience success in a world of self-sufficiency. Would I be bold enough to confront hubris of heart in my preaching?

Because of the missionary reality of tentmaking and bi-vocational ministry, my perception of the need for the application of the gospel has significantly deepened and it has quite obviously changed my preaching. I have been exposed to just how much further the pendulum can swing to the side of self-loathing or of self-love. I now better comprehend the accuracy of the Word of God to interpret and address these divergent realities that simultaneously exist in the lives of those who are listening when I preach. What a calling! What a privilege to preach the single, profound gospel of Jesus that is powerful and sufficient to save the wounded and self-hating, as well as the prideful and self-loving. Suddenly, my previously held conviction that the Word of God can simultaneously comfort and confront had expanded to new heights! Bi-vocationalism has convinced me all the more that I do not have to be creative to be persuasive.

KNOWLEDGE IS APPLICATION

The saying goes that knowledge is power. While that may be true in some settings of life, it is not true as regards our preaching and teaching of the Word of God. The Holy Spirit alone "is power." Our knowledge is not powerful. A better quip for those in ministry is that "knowledge is application." For the tentmaking or bi-vocational pastor, there are a preponderance of situations and realities we will gain knowledge of through our day job – things we could not have known outside of our vocational reality. These situations will radically expand the applicability of our Word ministry.

I have found increased applicational fodder – not as a result of my reading additional commentaries, nor from my scanning of media sources, nor by becoming a sophisticated poet or literature scholar. No. And thanks be to God – I don't have time for that. Rather, the daily straddling between the sacred and secular has expansively equipped me with profound applicational connections that have served my role as a pastor, preacher and missionary. This is not a replacement for studying the text of Scripture, but a complement to it. I can better translate the message to those in the world in which I live, work and play.

Examples

Because of this straddling, I now know what it is like to sit in meetings where corporate DEI values are presented, with employers who expect blanket endorsement regarding a critical theory lens on race, sexuality or gender. Though I have long known how pervasive these things are in the work environments of congregants in the culture of our world, my firsthand exposure has convinced me all the more of how potently I must preach the gospel of God's creational design in tandem with presenting the gospel of Christ's substitutionary atonement.

I now know what it is like to engage a person *with whom I work* about the faith, the inerrancy of Scripture, a biblical definition of gender or marriage, the reality of my own sin that is worthy of the wrath of God, and about how Jesus was more than just a good example. News flash: pastors do not typically have *work relationships* with nonbelievers or with those who hold vastly different interpretations of Scripture (though, sadly, this depends on how progressive is their church). Every pastor should have many relationships with apathetic or antagonistic individuals, which include their testifying to the hope of Christ and being willing to defend the kingdom of Jesus. However, I now know that it is vastly different to have these dialogues when it results in a weird vibe between you and a coworker with whom you daily work in close proximity. I have now seen how awkward and beautiful it is when a believer lashes out in anger in a work meeting, only to then ask for forgiveness from coworkers, acknowledging themselves a sinner who has received God's mercy. This is similar and yet altogether different than the volatile eruptions of anger and intimate moments of reconciliation inside of a pastor's office. These are things a bi-vocational or tentmaking pastor navigates *while serving as a pastor.*

I hope you get the point. There are a myriad of situations that surface when a tentmaking or bi-vocational pastor has one foot in the world and one foot in the church of Jesus. We are no more "in the world but not of the world" than those who serve Christ and His church from within a traditional ministry framework. However, our daily life in a vocation out in the world provides immense exposure that God can use to make our witness more contextualized and our preaching increasingly persuasive, for His glory and for His saving and sanctifying of those whom He would call to Himself.

Sometimes our exposures will be general, other times they will be acutely specific. This is true of ministry in general. For example, a pastor who has navigated a particularly unique situation in his own home, perhaps in his marriage or with his teenage children, will lean into that experience to help shepherd a family who is going through a similar experience. This does not mean that the application of the gospel and our ability to speak authoritatively from the Scriptures is mitigated or diminished if a pastor is not married or does not have teenage children. The Word of God is inherently applicable to homes in need of the gospel. However, where the Lord has providentially ordered parallel circumstances, there is great opportunity to acutely apply the Word – whether in a sermon, in a discipleship relationship, or in an evangelistic conversation.

This reality is amplified for the bi-vocational pastor who experiences increased exposures to life outside of the church. Even as I was writing the words of this chapter, a congregant asked for prayer for wisdom and boldness as he was privileged to speak before the governor and politicians in a public forum. This is a perfect example. For one, as his pastor I must pray for him, as he asked. As a shepherd, I should ask him about his anticipation or anxiety. For his encouragement, I should point him to Paul's wisdom and discernment among the philosophers of Athens in Acts 17, or to his confidence before governor Felix in Acts 23. What a platform that God ordains when he sets his servants before governors and kings! All this I should do and am thankful to do in the life of this brother, dominantly using the Word of God to share the truth of God. But more than that… because of my bi-vocational experience, it just so happens I can relate more acutely. I am able to share with him that the Lord had previously positioned me to speak before governors and politicians in a different state for a different purpose, when leading a housing nonprofit. This does not create a pastoral capacity to shepherd, but it helps.

Do not miss or minimize this if you are a bi-vocational or tentmaking pastor! Live boldly, preach boldly, and look for overlapping circumstances that will help you shepherd and serve the church of Jesus. Lead with specificity drawn from your experience in the kingdom of this world. Your hearers will benefit, so long as you are not platforming yourself. Platform your Maker and Redeemer. By the Spirit's help, persuade them to believe the gospel from the text you are declaring. More than that, pray that God would give you opportunities in your external vocation to apply what you are learning in your study, as you prepare to preach to the church. You just might be surprised at how powerfully the Word works, in two places at once.

A prayer for the bi-vocational minister, to this end:

O Lord, you have determined my allotted time and the boundaries of my life (Acts 17:26). Only because of your abundant goodness and redemptive mercy in Jesus am I able to stand with both of my feet squarely planted where you have sent me, unafraid and sufficient in the competence you give. Enable me to prioritize the work I do in your Word as holier and higher than all of my vocational tasks. Help me to understand the meaning of each text that I study, that I might preach Christ faithfully. Make me more faithful and persuasive. Help me to share your Word where I work in the world, and help the work I do in the world to transform how I preach your Word in your church. Embolden me in the places you have sent me, that I might speak the gospel with clarity, conviction and potency.
In Jesus name, and for His kingdom sake, Amen.

A prayer of Jesus for all of us, to this end:

[Father,] I have given them your word, and the world has hated them because they are not of the world, just as I am not of the world. I do not ask that you take them out of the world, but that you keep them from the evil one. They are not of the world, just as I am not of the world. Sanctify them in the truth; your word is truth. As you sent me into the world, so I have sent them into the world. And for their sake I consecrate myself, that they also may be sanctified in truth.
(John 17:14-19)

6

The Opportunity Cost

Considerations for the Church and Minister

Therefore, my beloved brothers, be steadfast, immovable,
always abounding in the work of the Lord, knowing that
in the Lord your labor is not in vain.
—1 Corinthians 15:58

For those whom the Lord calls to an intentional life of bi-vocational or tentmaking ministry, there is prospect of thriving – not merely surviving. We can declare with David:

> I believe that I shall look upon the goodness of the Lord in the land of the living! (Ps. 27:13)

In our daily lives in the land of the living, the construct itself presses us toward a posture of dependence, a mindset of mission, a confidence for plunder, and a litany of exposures to the world in which God would place His church for His kingdom's sake. This is the Lord's goodness, and it is full of opportunities for faith.

With every opportunity, however, there is a cost. It is important that we consider the opportunity cost of a boldly bi-vocational life.

Opportunity cost can be simply summarized as the value of what is lost, or not gained, when one chooses between two or more options. It is a basic principle used to valuate financial investments. For example, imagine that I am considering an investment in "X" – whether in real estate, a small business, or something else. In order to justify the wisdom of that investment, I must not only valuate the expected return from X, but the cost of no longer having the opportunity to invest the same resources into Y or Z. I lose whatever I could have gained if I had alternatively invested in Y or Z.

Opportunity cost applies to all of life.

When we go to bed early instead of staying up with friends or family, there is an opportunity cost. While I may feel energized the next morning, rising early to study or run on quiet streets, I also bear the cost of missing out on a conversation that would have deepened my understanding of someone I love. Or vice versa. If I stay up late to the benefit of relationships, I bear the opportunity cost of that decision when I cannot wake up early in the morning to study or run... or when I am miserable still trying to do so. That is just one example. Our lives are daily impacted by the opportunity cost of decisions or deferments across every category of life – relational, physical, financial, and even spiritual.

OPPORTUNITY COST IN THE
ECONOMY OF REDEMPTION

Opportunity cost is a core reality within the economy of God's kingdom. If we would grow in wisdom and maturity, part of our sanctification must include a valuation of the true impact of our obedience or disobedience, faith or fear, prayer or self-reliance. In our spiritual lives, when we give ourselves to something, anything, the return on our action or inaction is not merely the result of what we have done or not done. We must take into account what we could have alternatively done for the glory of God and the good of His kingdom.

For example, in His Sermon on the Mount, Jesus teaches:

> Therefore I tell you, do not be anxious about your life, what you will eat or what you will drink, nor about your body, what you will put on. Is not life more than food, and the body more than clothing? Look at the birds of the air: they neither sow nor reap nor gather into barns, and yet your heavenly Father feeds them. Are you not of more value than they? And which of you by being anxious can add a single hour to his span of life? (Matt. 6:25-27)

Jesus, we might say, is acknowledging the opportunity cost of anxiety. Jesus tells us that worry adds nothing to our lives. Not time, food or clothing. Not purpose. Nothing. Not only does worry rob us of joy and faithful living, it robs us of the opportunity to do something else in the very moment of our anxiety. If we are worrying, we are not worshiping. If we are worrying, we are not praying. If we are worrying, we are not working for the glory of God and the good of those who depend on us in the assignments given to us by God. Thus, if the Holy Spirit convicts us to repent of an hour of anxiety wherein we failed to trust our heavenly Father, we also must repent of what we could have gained with an hour of trusting and obeying. It is simple, really, but it is seismic in our spiritual lives.

This is one of the reasons that the church where I serve as pastor liturgically rehearses historic confessional prayers that acknowledge the obvious cost and the opportunity cost of our sin, before God. With a goal of habituating our hearts toward wholistic repentance and total trust in the merciful forgiveness of God, we pray in unison:

> Almighty God, our heavenly Father,
> We have sinned against you and against our fellow men,
> In thought and word and deed,
> *In the evil we have done*
> *And in the good we have not done,*
> Through ignorance, through weakness,
> Through our own deliberate fault.
> We are truly sorry and repent of all our sins.
> For the sake of your Son, Jesus Christ, who died for us,
> Forgive us all that is past;
> And grant that we may serve you in newness of life
> To the glory of your name.

Oh how often we must repent of the evil we have done and the good we have not done – *while we were doing the evil we should not have done*! To do so is to repent of the obvious cost as well as the opportunity cost of our sin – both for which Christ suffered and died.

SEEK FIRST THE KINGDOM OF HEAVEN

It is helpful for us to expand this concept beyond our sin. What of our attempts to steward our life as we invest in the kingdom of Jesus?

When we "seek first the kingdom of God and his righteousness" (Matt. 6:33) there is an opportunity cost to everything we do. There are paths we choose to take, and as a result, paths we can no longer take. We cannot take them both. If we say yes to a calling to plant a church, we say goodbye to those whom we have led, discipled, and taught in a different context. When we say yes to live in this neighborhood, we say no to the relationships and impact we may have made in a different neighborhood. The same is true as regards any role we play in the corporate world, in our social life, and in our parenting decisions. This is not complicated and it is quite obvious.

This should not lead us to paralysis. This is life.

Under the sovereign orchestration of our creator and redeemer, we steward our gifts, calling, time and lives. God has made it so that we can only do so in one place at a time. He made us such that we can only take one path and not another. We are not omnipresent, though He is and He sovereignly oversees our life for his ends. Our God, who is both omniscient and omnipresent, sees and cares for each of His children in the precisely allotted boundaries and days in which He has placed us (Acts 17:26). This means that if we seek first His kingdom and righteousness, we do not need to live in fear that the opportunity cost of a faith-filled decision to serve him over here and not over there will somehow minimize His return compared to if we had done the more visibly rewarding thing (by our measurement). No. We do not need to be anxious about failing to provide Him with a return on our investment when we seek first His kingdom! God is sovereign and merciful. He will receive glory when we seek His kingdom and His good! In His redemptive economy, there is always a return on the investments we make in faith.

> Therefore, my beloved brothers, be steadfast, immovable, always abounding in the work of the Lord, knowing that in the Lord your labor is not in vain (1 Cor. 15:58).

VALUATING THE COST OF BI-VOCATIONAL LIVING

If we would thoroughly evaluate the benefit of bi-vocational or tentmaking ministry, we must consider the opportunity costs (as well as the obvious costs) of formally having one foot in the church with the other foot vocationally planted outside of the church. While there is undeniable and beautiful return on such a diversified investment into the kingdom of God, it is a very different investment and return than if we were solely serving within the church. Where much is gained, much is given up.

Over my first decade in traditional ministry, I experienced many privileges that directly derived from full-time focused employment within the local church. While I was not aware of it at the time, the very construct enabled the blessings. I could spend fifteen to twenty hours each week preparing to preach. I had more time to read and study. I had capacity to schedule and arrange daytime shepherding meetings, as needs were revealed. I was able to make spontaneous house visits. I was able to stay home in the morning to serve my wife and young children, especially if I knew I would be out of the home for evening meetings. I was given study leave, without taking vacation. In summary, there was less chaos and more time. While very few pastoral tasks and privileges disappeared completely, tentmaking and bi-vocational ministry inherently made it so that most of these realities became less rhythmed and much less simple. There has been real opportunity cost.

Opportunity Costs

Three dominant opportunity costs are worthy of articulation and consideration.

The opportunity cost of reduced time and focus

Full-time employment outside of the church almost completely restricted my capacity to do extended study during daytime hours. My focused Word work occurred between 4:30 and 7am, before heading off to my "day job." The only alternative to this time block would have been late at night. Once I left the house, I entered an enterprise with rhythms and demands that were very foreign to what I had known in the church. In an effort to lead and advance our construction mission, each day included construction management, networking and fundraising appointments, Board engagement, as well as grant writing. Some weeks I was away from my family on work travel. It was different from any ministry environment I had previously known.

Thankfully, my normal rhythms included the privilege of interfacing strategic corporate leaders across larger cities in the Southeast – which included opportunities to pastor people outside of the church. However, I had minimal time, bandwidth, energy or margin to study the Word in preparation for pastoral opportunities within the local church. Sporadically I would attempt to arrive at a coffee shop forty-five minutes before a meeting, pulling out my Scriptures, sermon notes or a commentary. I would listen to audiobook readings of the text, chapter or book from which I was preaching (or other helpful resources) as I drove to and from work sites. I brought my sermon journal wherever I went, in the event of miscellaneous preaching thoughts and a few extra minutes showed up, unannounced. Focused study time in a "study" ceased to exist during that season of tentmaking.

The loss of time and bandwidth are significant opportunity costs for every bi-vocational and tentmaking pastor that I have known. The extent of the cost is impacted by the capacity of the individual to administrate a complex arrangement of time and tasks, as well as the nature of the outside employment – whether one is a truck driver, warehouse manager, coffee shop owner, barista, brewmaster, sales associate, financial advisor, corporate leader, or small-business owner.

The opportunity cost of a lack of availability
It is difficult for a multi-vocational minister to promptly respond to spontaneous shepherding needs within the church. After I had transitioned into a non-normative model of ministry, I found myself still capable of responding to urgent

crises (a death or accident, etc), but my ability to respond to lesser needs was delayed. It became normal and expected that I was not immediately available to receive phone calls. I let more calls go to voicemail, waiting to find a quiet moment and place to talk.

I realize that this describes a reality known to virtually every busy pastor, regardless of ministry construct. However, I felt an acute cost in comparison to the ease of response I had known when I was a "regular" pastor and church planter. It was harder. I began to notice that people in the church felt my bi-vocationalism. They realized that I was deployed by God outside of the church – and seeking to be respectful of my time, some people just assumed I was unavailable. This was not fully true. I was available, just less availably. [Ironically, my multiple jobs pushed against one another, preventing me from the suffocation and boundary-less workaholism I had known when working only "one job." As a result, I found myself having more time because I was not totally consumed by either vocational role. This is counterintuitive but has proven true over the last decade.]

Regardless if I felt I was less available or not, I began to find that my opportunities to deeply engage in ministry moments were reduced to heavier needs. I had to work harder to convey my desire and readiness to enter in. This is not a bad thing. It is just a real thing. In fact, this reality pushed against pastoral codependence that can develop, especially in a church plant or smaller church environment. It prompted a prioritization of a beautiful, biblical ecclesiology as the saints are equipped to minister among themselves. More on this in Chapter 7.

The opportunity cost of clarity (of priority)
A third opportunity cost that is worthy of emphasis is perhaps the most subtle. When one is solely employed by a local church

there is a singular "audience" or target of ministry – the local church. There are boundaries into which one is called. This is obvious, such that even people outside of the church see it. "You're the pastor of Christ Community Church, right? Your building is downtown, with the big blue sign, right?" If this is reality for the secular citizen, it should be abundantly clear to those who are called to minister in the local church. It is the command and design of God for the care of His people.

> Shepherd *the flock of God that is among you*, exercising oversight, not under compulsion, but willingly, as God would have you; not for shameful gain, but eagerly; not domineering over those in your charge, but being examples to the flock (1 Pet. 5:2-3, emphasis added).

For those who have been called into ministry, there should be no question as to the primary audience of our energy, gifts, time and focus. Our focus is not divided, though our time might be. Hebrews 13:17 makes plain that leaders will have to give an account for their ministry to *the church*.

> Obey your leaders and submit to them, for they are keeping watch over your souls, as those who will have to give an account. Let them do this with joy and not with groaning, for that would be of no advantage to you.

While there are connected target audiences of any ministerial life as we seek the welfare of the city in which God has placed us, the priority of one's calling and gifting is the local church where God has positioned His under-shepherds.

Here is the point. The prioritization of this reality is most easily experienced and understood when the boundary of one's vocational life directly overlays the local church where one is singularly employed. For the bi-vocational or tentmaking pastor, this reality does not go away. The priority of the local church must be understood and intensely guarded, complex as it may be. All this is to say that a bi-vocational life inherently comes with an opportunity cost of clarity (of priority). This is not something easily understood or felt by those outside of this ministry paradigm.

To be fair, the priorities within ministry are never easily navigated. All ministers of the gospel, regardless of paradigm, must daily make strategic decisions as regards how they will spend their time and steward their gifts. Prayer, wisdom, discernment and accountability are required. Sadly, many ministers of the gospel struggle to be good stewards of their time and gifts and too many churches suffer for it. If you are a full-time vocationally employed pastor – use every hour and moment you have been provided! May God be glorified as we steward the time He provides wisely and for His glory, for He is the one who orchestrated our placement for His purposes.

That said, it must be acknowledged that the "pull" of multiple sectors, employers or audiences is an inherent opportunity cost that comes with tentmaking or bi-vocational ministry.

Recently, I conversed with a bi-vocational church-planting pastor whose previous five years included twenty to fifty hours, weekly, working at a retailer of construction materials. While his heart and mission were about church planting and the individuals whom God was gathering, his days were dominantly filled with interactions among co-associates and customers. To be clear: his varying relational connections are not necessarily in competition with one another. He is living one life with a plethora of connections, all which can be funnelled toward his life calling as a church-planting pastor. However, he must accept and navigate the disproportionate relationship between his *time* and his *calling*. Much like a layleader in the local church, his time will be spent mostly with those who are either not convinced of the glory of God and the nature of His kingdom as revealed in Christ or who are not connected to his life as a kingdom-advancing church planter. Bi-vocational or tentmaking pastors must understand this and navigate it with humility. This perplexing reality is a profound opportunity cost.

The time demands, relational complexity, tyranny of the urgent, or actual contractual measurables of vocational deployment outside of the church *will significantly* impact one's experience within the church (unless you are an outlier with a rare arrangement). Distractions that complicate gospel ministry will not feel like distractions. Rather, they will feel like obligations – because they are. Again, this experience is consistent with what many laypersons feel when the deadlines and stresses of their work life hinder or obstruct their participation in many regular church realities. Let the bi-vocational or tentmaking pastor understand: one of the dominant opportunity costs of this construct is that the *primary* focus and calling of our life can feel like it is *not primary*.

STRENGTH IN WEAKNESS

For those called to this model of ministry, there will be days when our "outside" responsibilities build and we feel as though we can only conjure leftover energy in order to fulfill our priority ministry. This is hard, but real. Even on the good days that may be void of intensified conflict or trial, church realities can feel increasingly burdensome, simply because we are pulled in multiple directions. There will be ministry tasks, conversations and needs that must still be addressed, even if we cannot easily find the margin, capacity or strength to do so. It will be a fight, at times, to "boast" in this model of ministry. We can feel justified to minister with groaning, rather than with joy (contrary to the vision presented to us in Hebrews 13:17).

We must pray, daily, for spiritual maturity and discernment to remember that our life among the people of God is a divinely orchestrated priority, in spite of the rhythms that pull on us. It is critical that we surround ourselves with friends and disciples who understand the dynamic of our calling, the complexity of our time and space allotments (Acts 17:26), and who will remind us that ministering out of weakness is the design of God for the advancement of His kingdom.

The truth is, we *are* finite. We *are* exhausted. We *are* limited. We *are* weak. This is not simply a result of our ministry paradigm, rather it is true for all ambassadors of Jesus who would minister with His power and not our own. Weakness is the way. The Apostle Paul understood this:

> I will boast all the more gladly of my weaknesses, so that the power of Christ may rest upon me. For the sake of Christ, then, I am content with weaknesses, insults, hardships, persecutions, and calamities. For when I am weak, then I am strong (2 Cor. 12:9-10).

Indeed, the grace of God in Christ is sufficient for us, and His power is made perfect in our weakness. It is imperative that we soberly comprehend the complexity of our ministry construct so that when we experience the associated weariness, we are poised to lean into *His* strength, *His* peace, *His* purpose, and *His* rest. Strong faith is for weak people.

BECAUSE WE ARE WEAK...

Undeniably, our weakness in sin and in the flesh will bring other costs of bi-vocationalism to the surface. Or more accurately, we will experience certain costs more acutely because of how our remaining corruption intersects our model of ministry. A few of these costs are worthy of mention because they are so consequential. While our experience of these realities will differ according to individual spiritual maturity as well as our type of outside employment, they are worthy of articulation as they can adversely affect our souls, our ministries, and most importantly – our families.

By the grace of God, imperfect sinners are called and assigned to be shepherds, missionaries, and servants of Jesus and of His church. Gloriously, we are sanctified by His Spirit in and through our ministry assignments. But soberly, a call to ministry comes with spiritual assaults that provoke our flesh even as we seek to serve the Lord. For those who are given a bi-vocational or tentmaking assignment, there may be a strong temptation in three particular arenas – the allure of worldly success, the despair of failure, and the temptation of a divided life.

The Allure of Riches or Worldly Success
The desire for worldly comfort, riches and security is a temptation for many believers. Jesus exhorts us directly about this in His Sermon on the Mount:

> Do not lay up for yourselves treasures on earth, where moth and rust destroy and where thieves break in and steal, but lay up for yourselves treasures in heaven, where neither moth nor rust destroys and where thieves do not break in and steal. For where your treasure is, there your heart will be also …
>
> No one can serve two masters, for either he will hate the one and love the other, or he will be devoted to the one and despise the other. You cannot serve God and money (Matt. 6:19-21, 24).

Treasures on earth make for obsessions in the heart. It is not without reason that the apostle Paul transparently refers to his own struggle with covetousness as an example of the applicability of the Law. "For I would not have known what it is to covet if the law had not said, 'You shall not covet.' But sin, seizing an opportunity through the commandment, produced in me all kinds of covetousness" (Rom. 7:7-8). The desire to keep up with the Joneses and to feel self-secure is a remaining struggle for many believers who wrestle to trust in God as both redeemer and provider. Pastors, missionaries and vocational servants are not an exception. The wise words of Proverbs 30:7-9 make for a worthy prayer to the Lord our provider, aptly fitted for the life of vocationally deployed disciples.

> Two things I ask of you;
>   deny them not to me before I die:
> Remove far from me falsehood and lying;
>   give me neither poverty nor riches;
>   feed me with the food that is needful for me,
> lest I be full and deny you
>   and say, "Who is the Lord?"

When I ventured out from a traditional paradigm wherein my sole income had been from the local church, I needed the words of Proverbs 30 more than I had previously felt. I was faced with an intensified temptation to pursue worldly riches and success *because* I was suddenly working in the world. The temptation itself was not new. Rather, it was newly contextualized. I was now in the marketplace that monetarily rewarded excellence and punished mediocrity.

In God's providence, over the past decade I have experienced a measure of success outside of the church in the niche sector of nonprofit housing. In the earliest days of my vocational transition, I found myself suddenly navigating organizational growth, corporate partnerships as well as staffing and budget expansion. The allure of success presented itself to me in a different way than the familiar wrestling known to pastors in the subcultures of our churches and denominations. I knew that God was sovereign over all things, including the contextual factors that contributed to the organization's growth, but pragmatically, I was the one giving Board reports, media interviews, as well as receiving compensation bonuses. This was totally foreign to my previous experience of ministry success. Pastors don't receive compensation bonuses for delivering an excellent sermon or teaching series. My external vocation came with material benefits and public affirmation that were directly tied to performance. Suddenly my family was blessed with a modicum of discretionary resources that we had previously not known. We breathed a sigh of relief because, apparently, financial margin does feel like freedom. The pull toward self-sufficiency and worldly success was real.

A bi-vocational or tentmaking vocational paradigm is ripe for temptation toward the allure of riches and worldly success. For one, a secular corporation or sole proprietorship can provide a salary above and beyond what the local church could or perhaps should pay its ministers. Secondarily, the reward for faithful and effective performance is often tangible – the increase of material provision. This is not inherently problematic, but it is important to consider for those navigating a call into this vocational construct.

The biblical testimony suggests that the apostle Paul had a measure of financial security as a small-business owner.

While we know that he experienced additional provision, at times, from patrons like Phoebe (Rom. 16:2), his life as a missionary was dominantly sourced through a successful business as a tentmaker – so much so that he lived with freedom to travel as well as to host other disciples and followers. Consider the detailed description of his financial wherewithal given to us in the final verses of Acts. Luke writes:

> He lived there two whole years at his own expense, and welcomed all who came to him, proclaiming the kingdom

of God and teaching about the Lord Jesus Christ with all boldness and without hindrance (Acts 28:30-31).

I can only imagine that living at his own expense in Rome for two whole years was a tad different than enduring the cost of living in Ephesus. He had "made it" we might say. We get this. The cost of living in Johnson City is not the same as downtown Nashville.

When the Lord chooses to bless His tentmaking or bi-vocational servants with financial means and margin, it ought be graciously received for His glory and used for the good of the mission He has called us to. If this is your story, live it out in gratitude and faith – tithe and give of your offerings, investing in the kingdom with your resources as well as your model of ministry. Seek to remain vigilant to humbly wrestle through the temptations that come with such blessing. Repent when self-reliance, self-consuming or obsession over worldly treasure suffocates the freedom you have been given, and thus stifles your opportunity for obedience and ministry.

The Despair of Failure

There is a corresponding 'cost' to the allure of worldly success: the despair of failure. When there is *not* success in one's outside work and there remains difficulty to "live at our own expense" (as Luke described Paul's financial freedom), we can easily succumb to discouragement that can affect our soul, our home, and our zeal to minister in the local church.

Ministry is never not hard. The deceiver of the whole world makes war on those who keep the commandments of God and hold to the testimony of Jesus (Rev. 12:17). We should expect constant trial and temptation. More than that, it is God's design that in our weakness we would find His grace and strength to be sufficient. The Lord disciplines and sanctifies those He loves. Let the bi-vocational or tentmaking minister take note: the challenges of ministry can exponentially increase whenever we find ourselves *still* struggling to provide for our family even when we are sacrificially and strategically working two or more jobs.

It is of utmost importance to remember that the Word of God (and history, since) is rife with examples of burdened and even depressed ambassadors of Christ who lived their life desperate for the joy and hope promised in the gospel. We think of Charles Spurgeon, who on more than one occasion was willing to transparently share from the pulpit of London Metropolitan Tabernacle about the extremes of depression that he had known, as well as of his necessary reliance on Christ. He did not hesitate to write about his own despondency:

> Causeless depression cannot be reasoned with, nor can David's harp charm it away by sweet discoursings… The iron bolt which so mysteriously fastens the door of hope and holds our spirits in gloomy prison, needs a heavenly hand to push it back.[1]

Spurgeon is not an isolated example. We are reminded of David Brainerd, whose strategic and significant service to the Lord as a missionary to the Indians of the Northeast lasted only four short years. He died an early death at the age of twenty-nine in the home of Jonathan Edwards. In God's providence, in 1749 Jonathan Edwards published *The Life of David Brainerd,* a repository of riches in the form of a diary. God has since used Brainerd's meditations for His own glory and the good of countless missionaries and ministers. Brainerd was no stranger to suffering – be it physical or spiritual. In May 1743, he wrote: "My labor is hard and extremely difficult, and I have little experience of success to comfort me" – a reality amplified all the more by his loneliness: "I have no fellow Christian to whom

---

1   Charles Spurgeon, *Letters to My Students* (Grand Rapids, MI: Zondervan, 1972), p.163.

I might unbosom myself and lay open my spiritual sorrows, and with whom I might take sweet counsel in conversation about heavenly things."[2] He later wrote that "such fatigues and hardships as these serve to wean me more from the earth: and, I trust, will make heaven the sweeter ... and my eye is more to God for comfort."[3]

Indeed, a life of surrender in ministry is full of trial and weakness. Potently, the Apostle Paul testified to his own debilitating thorn:

> Three times I pleaded with the Lord that it should leave me. But he said to me, "My grace is sufficient for you, for my power is made perfect in weakness." Therefore I will boast all the more gladly of my weaknesses, so that the power of Christ may rest upon me (2 Cor. 12:8-9).

God is faithful to preserve the servants whom He calls, especially when it is hard and dark. If you are a minister of the gospel who has surrendered to a bi-vocational or tentmaking paradigm – the path will be full of trial, even as it is full of God's providential provision. Many brothers who have stepped out in faith in this arrangement have struggled to find employment that fits their gifts or their church arrangement. Many feel like they just do not fit; that they are neither "successful" in the ministry, nor are they proving to be "successful" in the marketplace. This is in addition to living without much margin. It can feel like constant failure. If this your experience, trust that you are not alone. May you embrace this cost as you keep surrendering to your calling, believing that He who is in you is greater than the one who is in the world – as well as

---

2 Jonathan Edwards, *An Account of the Life of the Reverend Mr. David Brainerd, in The Life of David Brainerd*, ed. Norman Pettit, vol. 7 of *The Works of Jonathan Edwards* (New Haven, CT: Yale University Press, 1985), p.207.

3 Ibid., p. 274.

the trial of this world. Do so daily. Trust that the Lord sustains those He assigns, with His strength and not our own. You are following the Chief Shepherd who suffered for your soul and for His church.

The Temptation of a Divided Life

A final "direct" cost or temptation associated with a bi-vocational or tentmaking life is common, to the point of being assumed. It is common not just among those who engage in a multi-vocational life, but among all of God's chosen exiles who are out of place in the kingdoms of this world. As citizens of the kingdom of heaven we are subjected to and often seduced by the common temptation of living a divided life. We live in the world, but we are not of the world (John 17:14).

For those whom God has called to vocationally straddle the sacred and the secular, we must remember that our sovereign King has sent us out as His ambassadors. Expect that you will navigate radically different cultural, moral, and ethical contexts – daily or weekly. Be aware of this challenge and embrace it as a means of affinity with the laypersons you pastor. For many, this is their constant reality – as they work for employers or authorities who may not submit, at all, to the glory and justice of God. This is what it is like for those whom you shepherd! Lord willing, they are anchored by the Word of God and the people of God, but they spend thousands of hours each year among coworkers who may live as though God is not worthy of worship and Christ is not needed for their salvation. You must be anchored just the same!

Commit to live a life of repentance wherever and whenever you see a divided life appearing, with disparate standards that are directly connected to where you are stationed. We do not live divided lives if we have Jesus as our King over every square inch of this world. Rehearse, again, the prayer of David in Psalm 86:11:

Teach me your way, O Lord,
  that I may walk in your truth;
  unite my heart to fear your name.

It must be our constant prayer that the Lord would give us undivided lives and hearts that fear His name as we walk in His truth in the places and roles where He has positioned us.

BENEFITS ALONG WITH THE COSTS

The opportunity costs and other more direct costs associated with a bi-vocational or tentmaking life are significant. They cannot be dismissed or minimized. To some, these costs will tip the scale toward a traditional paradigm of ministry. This is of God's design and it is a gift of discernment! To others, these costs will not be a deterrent. They may even serve as a motive for an increasingly bold facilitation of this boast-worthy model. Regardless, we must not fail to weigh these costs against the many blessings of this ministry paradigm. It is worthy of humble boasting!

In my own journey, the foot that has been squarely planted outside of the church has positioned me to grow in significant ways that I otherwise may not have experienced. It has been God's providence to mature my leadership inside of the church through experiences outside of the church – and vice versa. This continues every day. I have learned more acutely how to use my strengths, as well as how to recognize the burdensome nature of my weaknesses (that show up in every context). I have learned the necessity of surrounding myself with coworkers who have strengths where I am weak. I have learned how to manage multiple layers of employees, as well as when to delegate and how to provide support. I have been forced to make swift leadership decisions – whether in hiring, firing or ensuring financial stability. More than that, as an ambassador of Jesus, I have better learned how to contextualize the gospel and defend the faith from the Scriptures. These are not realities that I regularly navigated in the traditional pastorate – and they continue to serve me well both inside and outside of the church.

A prayer for the bi-vocational minister, to this end.

Almighty God and heavenly Father,
I have sinned against you and against my fellow men in thought and word and deed, in the evil I have done and in the good I have not done – through ignorance, through weakness, through my own deliberate fault, and I humbly repent. Thank you for laying the full cost and the opportunity costs of all of my sin on Jesus, my substitute. All the more, by your Spirit, help me to zealously invest in the kingdom of Jesus where you have positioned me, that I might boldly accept the opportunity costs of following in His mission. Enable me to be steadfast, immovable, always abounding in the work of the Lord, knowing that in the Lord my labor is never in vain.
In the name of Jesus, whose grace and strength are sufficient,
Amen.

7

The Balance

A Corrective Alignment

You then, my child, be strengthened by the grace that is in Christ Jesus, and what you have heard from me in the presence of many witnesses entrust to faithful men, who will be able to teach others also. Share in suffering as a good soldier of Christ Jesus... Think over what I say, for the Lord will give you understanding in everything.
—2 Timothy 2:1-3, 7

Alignment between every minister and the leadership of the church where he serves is of critical importance. This cannot be understated. Not only is this true as regards overall philosophy of ministry – including views on preaching, worship, evangelism, as well as the system of doctrine taught in the Scriptures – it is true with regard to how one fulfills their vocational assignment. Whether one is serving within a traditional vocational arrangement or a less common bi-vocational or tentmaking construct, this is of vital importance.

I recall a conversation with a pastor who was struggling in his ministry role as the full-time, solo pastor of a small rural church. While his ministry was 'inside the box' as a full-time pastor serving within a plurality of layelders, his self-described experience was very different than what I had previously known as a full-time pastor within the same denominational polity. I grimaced as I listened to him describe multiple examples of misalignment in his local setting. "During the week, church leadership drive by the church building to see if my car is in the parking lot. If it is not, they assume I am not working." This was hard to hear. There we were, sitting in a coffee shop, navigating his ecclesiastical, familial and financial challenges. We were talking about what he could do differently and more faithfully as a pastor and preacher. And yet, he was informing me that because he was not in the church office, "this doesn't count." This was only one of many examples of just how badly misalignment can hurt.

It is imperative that the local church and the minister(s) whom they employ are on the same page as regards how their vocational assignment can be faithfully fulfilled. What are the expectations as regards time, proximity, and presence? What are the shared understandings of accessibility – whether by text, by phone or in a church building? What frequency and tactic will be followed as regards home or hospital visits? What behaviors and ministry roles, if any, are expressly or subliminally expected to be fulfilled by the wife and children of a pastor?

These questions and their shared answers are profoundly important if there would be alignment in vocational fulfillment. This is true for traditional pastorates across diverse ministry contexts (rural/urban, large/small), as well as for churches and pastors navigating the uniquely sensitive boundaries of bi-vocational or tentmaking ministry.

ALIGNMENT AND ENDORSEMENT

Beyond alignment in vocational expectations, a healthy local church context necessitates an endorsement of the ministry model that is intentionally, strategically, and obediently being deployed. In the case of a bi-vocational or tentmaking ministry, the validity of the model must be understood and endorsed by local church elders and leaders who convey to their congregation the purposefulness and blessing of the arrangement.

A minister who is serving in a non-traditional, non-normative model should not be left alone to justify their construct and its strategic import for mission and ecclesiology. Rather, churches with bi-vocational or tentmaking ministers should be able to collectively, zealously boast in the Lord at the expansive ministry they are enabling. For this to happen, the elders and leadership of the body must thoughtfully craft the narrative that undergirds their localized expression of the paradigm – emphasizing both biblical permission and mission implications.

Regardless of the financial or hourly arrangement, the narrative is *not* that "we have a part-time pastor who is unfortunately busy or distracted from the ministry." Rather, "we have a full-time minister of the gospel and under-shepherd of Christ whom we are thankful is able to serve our body with gifts given by God, even as we intentionally release him into our city for the advancement of the kingdom of God!" The sending church is positioned to trust that God will provide for them through this model, even as they trust their minister to manage his time, calling, and family – in complicated overlapping roles.

THE OPPORTUNITY COSTS FOR THE
LOCAL CHURCH

As intentional as this model should be and as effective as it can be, the reality is that when a local church releases their minister to serve outside of the church there is an opportunity cost for the church. A church must count the cost of having a shepherd with dual internal and external outlets of ministry. The arrangement will inherently impact internal church culture and rhythms, the roles of the elders, deacons and other staff, as well as the congregational interactions with their dually employed pastor. A church *will* have a minister(s) whose time and energy may appear, to some, to be divided. Their pastor's car will not always be in the parking lot.

Flexibility will be required for meetings and communications. Office hours may be limited. Teaching outlets and opportunities may need to be reduced compared to a traditionally-employed pastor. And yet, depending on the type of outside work, none of these realities may materialize. In fact, if a pastor also serves as an author, counselor, seminary professor, or accountant – much of his "other" work may be literally accomplished within the church building. In full candor, this has been my experience. While, at times, I have needed to travel for nonprofit consulting or strategic meetings, virtually all of my grant writing and video calls have occurred within my office at the church building. The same is true for our bi-vocational pastoral intern, whom we are currently watching God raise up in our midst. His complementary job outside of the church is dominantly accomplished inside of the physical church. When this occurs, it understandably appears less divided and is altogether different than the time and space reality for a bi-vocational minister who might be employed in a corporate, retail, educational, manufacturing or transportation space.

Because the contextual uniqueness of each bi-vocational arrangement is the factor that most directly impacts the experience for a sending church, it is requisite that church elders and leaders name and embrace the specific opportunity costs that impact their local setting. Many of the costs referenced in chapter 6 (in relation to the minister) correlate with opportunity costs for the sending church. It is incumbent upon church leadership to investigate, articulate, and accept these costs, not only for the sake of accountability for the minister whom they employ, but so that they are able to lead the congregation to embrace the opportunity costs of the model. There are profound missional, financial and contextual benefits that the leadership of the church believe outweigh the opportunity costs! A sending congregation must understand that the costs, real as they are, have not been determined by church leadership to outweigh the reward or to mitigate the impact of the local church's mission.

Actually, it is more than this. Church leadership can be encouraged that a tentmaking or bi-vocational ministry construct may also be used by God to provide a subtle yet significant corrective to unbiblical or unwise pastoral realities that repeatedly inflict the local church.

A SUBTLE, GENTLE CORRECTIVE

There are common struggles that many pastors face in their leadership of the local church. Common does not mean universal. It would be unwise to imply that every minister or every church battles identical challenges. We do not. Just as we are uniquely gifted and equipped by God with diverse capacities to invest in His redemptive economy, we are unique sinners who need God's mercy and power to sanctify us as we face varying trigger temptations. Some pastors struggle with depression and self-doubt, others with pride and self-love.

Some dominantly with the passion of lust or anger, others with fear or apathy.

Just as we are similar but different in our experience of sanctification, we face similar but different challenges in our contextual and local environments. Any minister of the gospel who has served in different churches, whether they are across the world or down the street from one another, knows that the trials in ministry are never precisely duplicated. And yet, as different as they are, we still share the same reality. We are exiles and sojourners, not at home in this world that is yet to be fully redeemed. The people of God have known common struggles, collectively and individually, throughout the history of redemption (see 1 Cor. 10:6-13). With the saints who have gone before, we fight battles against a common enemy with hearts that have known common temptations.

SOME ELEPHANTS IN THE CHURCH

Despite the commonalities, however, the church somehow keeps being surprised by repeat struggles, specifically as regards pastoral leadership. There are elephants in the church that we must not fail to notice. To be fair, I am encouraged that the church is increasingly acknowledging many of these mammoth challenges more directly and judiciously. Issues such as pastoral bullying, abuse of authority, pastoral isolation and ministerial mediocrity have been increasingly written about, talked about, and in some cases, publicly exposed.[1]

It is not my intent to thoroughly diagnose, correct or administer the salve of the gospel for churches broken by certain leadership challenges. Rather, the contribution I

---

1 Paul David Tripp, *Dangerous Calling: Confronting the Unique Challenges of Pastoral Ministry* (Wheaton, IL: Crossway, 2012). Michael J. Kruger, *Bully Pulpit: Confronting the Problem of Spiritual Abuse in the Church* (Grand Rapids, MI: Zondervan Reflective, 2022)

desire to make in this discussion is to reference how a boldly bi-vocational paradigm of ministry can indirectly, and surprisingly, help address these repetitious realities – even offering a vocational hedge of protection. To a few of these sober realities we now turn.

Laziness and Lack of Quality
The local church should be the last place on earth that succumbs to leadership laziness and a shoddy standard of "good enough" for the things that we do. We are called to be ambassadors of Jesus in all that we do. Our teaching, preaching, hospitality, counseling, music, community engagement and stewardship ought to be done for the glory of the God whose image and redemption we reflect. As Paul writes to the men and women in the church at Colossae,

> Bondservants, obey in everything those who are your earthly masters, not by way of eye-service, as people-pleasers, but with sincerity of heart, fearing the Lord. Whatever you do, work heartily, as for the Lord and not for men, knowing that from the Lord you will receive the inheritance as your reward. You are serving the Lord Christ (Col. 3:22-24).

These words are directive and universally germane to individuals in every church across time and place, regardless of station or status in life. Sadly, they are not always heeded – by laity *or by ministers of the gospel*. When I transitioned from pastoral ministry to the nonprofit housing sector, I suddenly found myself orchestrating a home repair enterprise that included thousands of volunteers annually. What I observed in that process confirmed what I had already experienced in the local church. The nobility of a "good work" (whether an act of service or an act of leadership; whether accomplished by a volunteer or in a vocation) often comes with the temptation to settle for mediocrity. We can be content to merely feel good about what we are doing, even if what we have actually done is only "good enough." To say it differently: when we are doing something good, there is a pull to find worth in *what* we are doing rather than considering the worthiness of *how* we are doing the thing(s) that we are doing.   But it matters.

The church of Jesus represents His inaugurated new creation on His earth. We simply must not settle for mediocrity – for laziness or shoddy effort at any of the tasks He calls us to! I am not implying that we must perform for God or for others. Not in the least. Nor am I insinuating that we must become experts or professionals if we would be effective in the ministry to which we have been called. No. We can and must only minister out of humility and weakness, that we might find His strength to be sufficient. That said, however, we must give of our whole selves to the work we have been called, seeking vigilantly to make progress in all of our kingdom efforts.

We need to repeatedly internalize what Paul exhorted Timothy:

> Practice these things, immerse yourself in them, so that all may see your progress. Keep a close watch on yourself and on the teaching. Persist in this, for by so doing you will save both yourself and your hearers (1 Tim. 4:15-16).

We must persistently and progressively labor to strategize, organize, prioritize and actualize our efforts to the best of our redeemed capacity. This is the expectation of all whom the Lord calls to minister on behalf of Christ in the local church, regardless of their task – teaching, preaching, counseling, or serving.

> "If your heart is in functional awe of the glory of God, then there will be no place in your heart for poorly prepared, badly delivered, functional pastoral mediocrity… I think we should

all be shocked at the level of mediocrity that we tolerate in the life and ministry of the local church."[2]

How is it that we could possibly settle for mediocre ministry? The apostle Paul's appeal to the church and testimony of his own life directly confronts this.

> Do you not know that in a race all the runners run, but only one receives the prize? So run that you may obtain it. Every athlete exercises self-control in all things. They do it to receive a perishable wreath, but we an imperishable. So I do not run aimlessly; I do not box as one beating the air. But I discipline my body and keep it under control, lest after preaching to others I myself should be disqualified (1 Cor. 9:24-27).

Again, Paul reminded Timothy: "It is the hard-working farmer who ought to have the first share of the crops. Think over what I say, for the Lord will give you understanding in everything" (2 Tim. 2:6-7).

Bi-vocational ministry gives us the opportunity to think over these things. In fact, if we would navigate our dual calling with effectiveness and unto sustainability, then we *must* think on these things. When we do, we make a simple but profound discovery. Our calling to serve God inside of the church requires that we serve Him excellently outside of His church, and our calling to serve Him outside of the church demands that we serve Him excellently within His church. Bi-vocational ministry can provide a functional corrective to laziness, mediocrity and settling for a "good enough" effort in ministry. It is not for the faint of heart.

Consider that within the transactional world of secular employment, it is expected that individuals will fulfill their

---

2 Paul David Tripp, *Dangerous Calling: Confronting the Unique Challenges of Pastoral Ministry* (Wheaton, IL: Crossway, 2012), p.141.

responsibilities in such a way as to satisfy their earthly employer. Even those who do not fear God know that much is to be gained if they impress those who pay them and who might praise them before others. This is the way of the world. Thanks be to God that the church on earth does not live by such a performative transactional arrangement! We must not – for we have been saved by grace alone through faith alone in the performance of Jesus alone. Thus, all that we do must be motivated by gratitude to God and in reflection of His redeeming glory.

Does His mercy give permission for mediocrity, however? No! Does the work of ministry, motivated by gratitude for God's grace and zeal for His glory, come with more laziness and procrastination and distraction than work that is motivated by money or any other transactional return? May it not be! How backward is it, then, if in *this* kind of performative and transactional world, the church of Jesus lets off an aura of unpreparedness, lack of strategy, lack of urgency, integrity, creativity (authorized), accountability or excellence? We must not settle for "good enough" when we are serving Him who gave up His life for us.

Consider this. Are believers in the body of Christ generally *more* strategic in their investing in the local church or in the corporation or business that employs them? I am not speaking of capacity of time for investment, I am speaking of strategic intent to do so. Are Christian businessmen generally more urgent and less lazy in their development of employees at work, or in their spiritual discipleship and shepherding of their family at home? Many maturing Christian executives have humbly groaned in repentance: "At work." Why is this? Because the accountabilities and expectations of their earthly employer *appear to be* more consequential than their ecclesiastical and spiritual life. But it is not so!

For those called to serve in a bi-vocationalism or tentmaking ministry, the paradigm itself can push against this. It provides the opportunity for servants of the gospel to observe their own work ethic, standards of excellence, and strategic service in multiple sectors, simultaneously. A bi-vocational pastor must not work more laboriously or strategically for an earthly master in their day job than they do for the Lord in His church. We serve the same Master in both spheres! There cannot be a dual standard. We must live with undivided hearts and lives (Ps. 86:11). Thus, it is for our good that one role/vocation will affect and reflect the other.

The apostle Paul was a man with ridiculous zeal. Passion, intensity and urgency described his entire life – his pre-conversion self as an angry persecutor of the church and his new creation self as a church-planting apostle of Jesus. Do we expect that he operated with any less zeal, vigilance, strategic-mindedness, and urgency as a business owner? Did he settle for making shoddy tents just to get by or in an effort to increase his profit margin? Surely not. Conversely, does Scripture hint that he gave himself to producing high-end tents and growing his business, only to settle for "good enough" sermons, apostolic counseling appointments or church-planting efforts? No! He was the same redeemed man, pursuing a worshipful standard of excellence in all that he did.

If Paul would effectively produce and sell quality tents in the marketplace of Athens, by necessity he had to give himself to delivering prepared and persuasive gospel messages to the secular philosophers who were engaging him *in the same marketplace.* His reputation as a tentmaker served his role as a preacher, and his reputation as a confident communicator and preacher of the gospel earned respect among those would buy his tents.

Bi-vocational and tentmaking ministry can necessarily serve as a helpful corrective to mediocrity, laziness and "good enough" efforts in the church – deepening our conviction that there is great return on our investment when we seek excellence for the glory of God in all that we do.

Lack of Boundaries

Another struggle in vocational ministry that can be helpfully addressed through a bi-vocational paradigm is a lack of boundaries. This seems counterintuitive. Does not the addition of an added vocational assignment make the single servant of God more prone to a boundary-less existence? Surprisingly, it does not. If a minister of the gospel is called by God to responsibly serve in differing sectors of His kingdom, both inside and outside of His church, there must be boundaries that are both established and respected for the sake of effectiveness and sanity.

Boundaries are needed for all who are called by God to serve in ministry. We are finite in our capacity – with limited time, energy and resources with which to serve Christ in His kingdom. We can only be in one place at a time. We must stop doing one thing so that we can start doing another. We must transition from focusing on a shepherding need in the church if we would engage the shepherding opportunities awaiting us when we drive up our driveway.

A common struggle that plagues many pastors is the inability to intentionally establish personal and familial boundaries with the local church. Ministry can consume. It dangerously becomes an obsession that oppresses the mind and affects the body. It has been called a mistress, seductively alluring faithful husbands away from the wife of their youth as they fixate on the bride that belongs to Christ. It is a significant challenge for ministers and missionaries to establish mental, physical, emotional, relational and calendrical boundaries. We must urgently and responsibly do so, lest we think of ourselves as anyone's savior, provider or messiah. Thanks be to God, we are not.

While many pastors struggle to establish self-imposed boundaries, it is equally common for members within the church to function as if their pastor and his family do not need (or should not have) any boundaries. Others are simply unaware when they are crossing boundaries that may exist. In our age of instant connection, this is a significant trial that inflicts the homes of ministry families.

The risk of ministry intrusion can be a constant burden, showing up unannounced as suddenly as a text alert. Whether we are at the dinner table with our family, at a child's recital or athletic event, or sitting on the porch swing reading a book beside our spouse – a text notification can instantaneously redirect our moment, our mind and the objects of our affection. We read the text, and we cannot unread it, try as we may. Sometimes these communications are critical and worthy of immediate response. Other times, they arrive because someone in our church read an article they thought their pastor might enjoy. Or, they had a random idea and "you were the first person I thought of." I am likely not the sole recipient of a text message or voicemail recording that begins with: "I know you're on vacation, but I was just thinking…" Did they listen to my voice recording redirecting them to one of our other pastoral staff while I am away?

Minister of the gospel, be brave to share with those you lead the importance of your family time, evening boundaries, and even the nature of your personal struggle to "turn it off" and shepherd the flock of God in your own home. Whenever I have needed to courageously remind congregants that I am away camping with my family, that "it can wait," and that I struggle to keep my mind and heart fixed on my family above the ministry – those interactions have been beautiful. Church members have prayed for me in the moment, asked for forgiveness for insensitivity, redirected their inquiry to a different pastor or elder – and God has been gracious to mature both pastor and congregation alike. Brothers, be vigilant in this!

Modern ministry in a culture of immediate gratification – with lesser awareness of others – requires that under-shepherds of Jesus establish clear vocational boundaries for our life and family. Once again, a bold bi-vocational model of ministry can surprisingly help with this. A dually employed individual must clarify with both their local church leadership as well as their external employers how they will responsibly fulfill their many diverse responsibilities. Without clearly articulated boundaries, the construct will fall to the ground, leaving a burned-out minister and his family sitting on a pile of unmet expectations.

As mentioned previously, my life as a bi-vocational pastor has shockingly made me feel less busy, not more. Even as the scope of my responsibilities have expanded in both my pastoral and non-church roles, I am less consumed now than I was when serving as a solo church planter with significantly less people and needs to serve. Why is that? There are multiple reasons, to be sure. But one significant reason is that the boundaries required in this bi-vocational life have caused both "jobs" to press against one another, thus keeping ministry from squashing my soul or my family. The responsibilities of the two roles have been significant enough that they have required order and boundaries that prevent either role from overreach and oppressive consumption.

A bi-vocational construct, with its myriad of responsibilities, has enabled many burdened ministers of the gospel to learn that we *can* set "this" down. Whatever "this" is. We can let it go for a moment, or for this evening or for the rest of this week. In fact, we *must*. We *must* be able to release our grip on ministry burdens, tasks or plans so that we might find capacity to invest in other responsibilities that the Lord has ordained for this moment, or for this evening or for the rest of the week. And when we do, with faith-filled dependence on the God who holds all things together, we experience a freedom *in* ministry and *from* ministry that propels us to wholeheartedly and dependently invest in the place where God has most fundamentally assigned our shepherding – at home.

Shepherd, your bi-vocational construct can ironically bring boundaries and freedom that aligns with your primary calling – to pastor shepherd the flock in your own home.

UNBURDENED BY BIBLICAL POLITY

There is a final constellation of challenges worthy of discussion which bi-vocationalism can effectively address when it is boldly facilitated through a healthy, biblical polity of church governance.

Many pastors navigate the trials of ministry, alone. Those who serve and lead smaller congregations feel the responsibility for preaching, teaching, counseling, training, visiting, janitoring, evangelizing, discipling, scheduling, and administering church life. In the majority of ministry contexts, pastors are required to be a jack-of-all-trades who often feel like a master of none. It is daunting, isolating, and burdensome.

More troubling is if pastor jack-of-all-trades is perceived by others to be a master of most; or worse, if he thinks this of himself. If a minister of the gospel is gifted in preaching, relating, visioning, writing, leading, and organizing – there begins to form an expectation for a scaled influence. In an age of social influencers and celebrity pastors, this can lead to tremendously unhealthy leadership environments.

It is worthy to articulate, yet again, that the Lord assigns spheres of influence for all whom He calls for His glory and for the advancement of His kingdom (2 Cor. 10:13). In His perfect providence, at certain times and in certain ways, the Lord positions select servants to have tremendous influence, at a scale that must not be normalized nor is it often duplicated. Thanks be to God for those whom He positions and preserves through such visible and influential assignments. We ought to pray for them, their ministries, and their ministry accountabilities more than we do; and certainly more than we celebrate them.

The challenge lies in the observable reality that the local church, in disparate contexts, repeatedly orbits around the gifts and personality of a single servant of God. The church frequently and often literally sets individual servants of God on a stage, under the lights – often in rooms that don't require a platform or need the extra lighting. More than that, social media and podcast platforms enable Christian disciples to scroll through the litany of leaders whom they admire, picking and choosing the voice that will dominantly influence their spiritual life and perhaps trajectory. A voice of influence that is void of relationship.

The Scriptures clearly articulate that the local church is not to be led by an individual shepherd, even if he is pastor jack-of-most-trades. Christ alone is the head of the body, the Chief Shepherd of His church. Under-shepherds of Christ are to serve in a plurality to make this plain.

Acts 14:21-23 records how Paul and Barnabas went about preaching the gospel and planting a plurality of elders in each church that God had planted.

> When they had preached the gospel to that city and had made many disciples, they returned to Lystra and to Iconium and to Antioch, strengthening the souls of the disciples, encouraging them to continue in the faith, and saying that through many

tribulations we must enter the kingdom of God. And when they had appointed elders for them in every church, with prayer and fasting they committed them to the Lord in whom they had believed.

What does a plurality of elders have to do with bi-vocationalism? Everything. To put it simply, a boldly bi-vocational model of ministry necessitates a biblical polity with an active and functionally designed plurality of elders, which then mitigates the risk of the local church celebrating and granting excess influence to any one individual pastor.

The model itself uniquely positions a competent leader and servant of God to use his gift set in an *increasingly* influential way, with a measure of *decreased* visibility. This is beautiful and profoundly freeing. In practice, bi-vocationalism ensures that there are *many* moments when a minister's use of his gifts remain unseen by those in the church – because they are being deployed outside of the church (but inside of the kingdom of God). As a result, an individual servant is less likely to receive unwise celebrity status or garner undue influence. This is sensible, for he is serving (or leading) in places where there are no stages or lights. This is not to say that there is no accountability or oversight. That is a different reality. The point is that, outside of rare exceptions, a faithful bi-vocational arrangement generally gives the influence-fixated church less reason to notice or to cheer.

For this to occur, there needs to be healthy, purposeful plurality of elders who will jointly lead the local church, according to biblical design, rather than relying on the usefulness of any one particular servant.

Bi-vocational or tentmaking ministry, when boldly implemented within biblical parameters, will instigate the adoption of a biblical polity and a team approach to ministry. Often, churches with a plurality of elders can fall prey to operating mostly as a board of directors. They are just another committee entrusted with the business of the church. This is not God's design and nor will it work in a boldly bi-vocational paradigm. The model itself *necessitates* that the church intentionally raise up elders (*presbyteros* – "pastors") with complementary strengths that align for the sake of mission, as well as that God uses to address individual weaknesses. Specific shepherding roles ought be given and expected of various elders, so that their bi-vocational pastor(s) can steward their best gifts both inside and outside of the church.

In other words, a church with a healthy and bold bi-vocational vision is less likely to orbit around the gifts of one, sharing shepherding tasks visibly in such a way that dilutes the influence and charisma of any one leader.

This is in keeping with the role distribution that undergirds the redemptive plan of God:

> And he gave the apostles, the prophets, the evangelists, the shepherds and teachers, to equip the saints for the work of ministry, for building up the body of Christ (Eph. 4:11-12).

The local church will be more effective and visibly built up for the work of ministry when the diversity of gifts and roles among under-shepherds are shared in such a way as to reduce the social influence of any one shepherd. While this is true for churches with a traditionally employed vocational pastor (or pastoral staff), it is essential for a bi-vocational ministry setting.

Where there is an intentional plurality, there can be a strategic maximization of the unique strengths and gifts of each elder/shepherd for the glory of God and the expansion of His kingdom. In the case of a bi-vocational pastor, he is more enabled to steward his dominant strengths and divine gifts in a unique calling that is both inside and outside of the church – with less visibility or celebration by the church; and Lord willing, with more influence for Jesus's sake in the city where he has been sent.

A WORD OF CAUTION

It is important to understand that bi-vocational or tentmaking ministry does not inherently address these challenges or bring corrective alignment. In fact, the construct conceivably could produce more mediocrity and laziness as we throw things together last minute in light of our vocational demands. Through the complexity of this life, we can easily become "soldiers who get entangled by civilian pursuits" (2 Tim. 2:4) such that distraction or mediocrity become the norm. More than that, we could be increasingly prone to suffer oppression-by-ministry, as our calling inside and outside the church consumes us with despairing obligations or an adventurous sense of thrill. Dangerously, our multiple roles and any resulting visibility could cause us to think too highly of ourselves and our social influence, especially if others treat us as omnicompetent due to our dual investment in both the church and the marketplace.

Let the minister take caution. The call to bold bi-vocationalism requires humility, repentance and faith, that through it the Spirit of God would bring alignment to His revealed will for those who serve Him in this way. Through it, may God tether our hearts that can too easily settle for mediocrity or selfishly seek the celebration of others. Through it, may the church of Jesus be built up and may the Spirit of God bring health to your soul, your marriage, and your family.

A prayer for the bi-vocational minister, to this end:

Jesus the Chief Shepherd,
You alone know your sheep, and your sheep know your voice. Enable
the under-shepherds of your church to speak, lead and influence in
such a way that it is your voice that your people hear, and not our
own. In the daunting task of shepherding, protect me from settling
for mediocrity and laziness, as well as from suffocating oppression
and boundary-less obsession. Raise up a faithful plurality of elders
and leaders in your church who are complementarily called and
gifted for the shared task – using their dominant strengths in the
outlets you have ordained from before time. Grant me wisdom,
balance, accountability and excellence as I fulfill this single life of
calling inside and outside of your church, for the influence of your
name alone. Grant sustainable strength and health for my family for
as long as you would call me to this duality. Do so for your glory in
a healthy church with bold under-shepherds who share in this life
with me. For the sake of your name, Amen.

The Vision

Something Even Bigger

Then comes the end, when he delivers the kingdom to God the Father after destroying every rule and every authority and power. For he must reign until he has put all his enemies under his feet.
—1 Corinthians 15:24-25

There remains much to be said to the church about strategic bi-vocational and tentmaking ministry and its contextual implementation in the various assignments given us by God. In each instance there are innumerable variables of significant import. These realities stack upon one another, uniquely, in each case. Undoubtedly the health of each bi-vocational arrangement depends on the biblical orthodoxy of the sending church, the spiritual maturity and health of the pastor and his family, the execution of the model from within a biblical polity, the strategic sharing of the shepherding burden by other elders, as well as the endorsement of the local congregation. Even more, the effectiveness of the model will be impacted by the rhythms and type of external work, the alignment with pastoral gifts and capacity, not to mention the needs in the local community that is being served by the external vocation. These, and many other actualities, influence just how faithful and sustainable a boldly bi-vocational life can be.

Because of the distinctiveness of each instance, the church ultimately needs something more fundamental than catalytic conversations, conferences or books (even this one) about how to contextualize tentmaking, bi-vocational or co-vocational ministry – or whatever the next semantic may be. In God's providence, I did not pursue this ecclesiastical shift because of a compelling argument found in a book, podcast or conference. Rather, the Lord interrupted my traditional life of ministry in a surprising way. The Holy Spirit sustained us through a convicting season of curiosity that included a renewed searching of Scripture, a constant measure of support from my wife and family, as well as a deep churning until the Lord made our bi-vocational arrangement clear. From the beginning, the sojourn has included much duress and new exposures of weakness that have been met with the Lord's strength. I have discovered the providence of God to be perfect, always and in every way, even when it does not feel like it. But again, this is merely my own experience.

Because every bi-vocational calling is contextually unique, personally informed, as well as spiritually complex, it would be unfortunate if the preceding pages have only served to platform a non-normative ministry paradigm as though it were something every reader should lean toward. This is not the way that Scripture presents tentmaking or its younger half-sibling. It is not for everyone, nor is it in need of a marketing campaign. What is needed, rather, is for those who are called to tentmaking or bi-vocational ministry to boldly pursue their calling and assignment from God from within a larger, biblical vision of the kingdom of God that has broken into the kingdom of this world in Christ. The kingdom of heaven has indeed come down to earth in Jesus – with all authority, for all obedience, unto all the nations, in fulfillment of all the prophets. Every calling and every conversation about vocational calling resides within that vision.

A FRAMEWORK WITHIN A FRAMEWORK

In an effort to biblically understand any reality or issue as it relates to the people of God, we must do more than search Scripture for references to *that* particular institution, practice, behavior, or attitude. Rather, we must consider how that particular reality is informed by all of what God has declared. If we would understand God's creational design and redemptive purpose for marriage, for example, we must not limit the scope of our scriptural study to passages *about* marriage or the role of husband or wife. Rather, we must consider the whole counsel of God that records His design from creation for all who have been made in His image, namely His glory. The glory of God as the chief end of man – every man and woman – fundamentally impacts every relationship among them, most dominantly marriage! Thus, we must trust that the whole of God's Word which teaches us of His holiness, His sovereignty, His rescuing us in Christ, and His transforming our identity into a holy people – is foundational for every biblically tethered marriage.

We must wisely navigate every ecclesial, missional and pastoral issue from within a framework that is larger than the actual issue. The Word of God presents a wholistic framework of life "under the sun" for the people of God who "search out by wisdom all that is done under heaven" (Eccl. 1:13). When, by wisdom, we apply ourselves to comprehend the design of God, the redemption of God, and all of the promises of God – we find expansive purpose in all that we do. This includes our individual and familial experience of vocational ministry and manner by which the Lord provides for our material needs.

> He has made everything beautiful in its time. Also, he has put eternity into man's heart, yet so that he cannot find out what God has done from the beginning to the end. I perceived that there is nothing better for them than to be joyful and to do good as long as they live; also that everyone should eat and drink and take pleasure in all his toil – this is God's gift to man. I perceived that whatever God does endures forever; nothing can be added to it, nor anything taken from it. God has done it, so that people fear before him (Eccles.. 3:11-14).

The Preacher in Ecclesiastes wisely and repeatedly rehearses the truth that in this life under the sun, all that we do is before God. If we understand this, nothing is vanity. If we do not, all is but a vapor. But it is not. We can and we should go about "eating our bread with joy and drinking our wine with a merry heart," trusting that God [in the gospel] has already approved of what we do (Eccles. 9:7). The point of the matter is that we must fear God and keep His commandments in all that we do, "for this is the whole duty of man" (Eccles. 13:13).

If we believe that our vocational calling comes from the God who created us, redeemed us and assigned to us spheres of influence with allotted boundaries in time and space for His glory, then we can joyously and sacrificially fulfill our duty while we daily live under the sun with myriad responsibilities and opportunities. We can do so trusting that all things under heaven will accomplish the purpose God intends. This is a bigger vision that must overwhelm every minister of the gospel, regardless of their vocational paradigm.

If you are a tentmaking or bi-vocational pastor, may you have a panoramic vision of the kingdom of God inside of which the church of God and individual servants of God play an ordained role. We must fix our eyes on Jesus (Heb. 12:2), who alone is in the center of the picture of the kingdom of God. When we expand the frame out, pictured for us is the glory of His kingdom and reign from eternity and unto forever.

AN UNSHRINKABLE VISION

There will always be reason to focus our sight on our own heart, home, church, city and life of vocational ministry. We should long to *see* the kingdom come on earth as it is in heaven *in those places.* However, "God purposed that the borders of our vision be much, much larger than the boundaries of our lives. We were meant to see more than our physical eyes can see, and it is that greater vision that was meant to engage, excite, connect, and satisfy us."[1]

Before His ascension, consider how Jesus both corrects the near-sightedness of His disciples as well as expands the scope of their vision. The eleven had just experienced the greatest forty days in the history of the world. They sensed that the moment had arrived for something even greater.

> So when they had come together, they asked him, "Lord, are you at this time going to restore the kingdom to Israel?" He said to them: "It is not for you to know the times or dates the Father has set by his own authority. But you will receive power when the Holy Spirit comes on you; and you will be my witnesses in Jerusalem, and in all Judea and Samaria, and to the end of the earth" (Acts 1:6-8).

Ironically, though they anticipated the culmination of the kingdom, their question inherently minimized it to a narrow place and time. Their vision of a nationalistic kingdom with

---

1 Paul David Tripp, *A Quest for More: Living For Something Bigger Than You* (Greensboro, NC: New Growth Press, 2007), p.16

geographic boundaries was too small. They were yet to grasp that the rule of the kingdom of Jesus was never intended to be narrowed to Israel. From eternity, the kingdom of God was set to extend from Israel to the ends of the earth. The very earth where all creatures and creation itself has groaned for freedom and release from the decay of death.

> For the creation was subjected to frustration, not by its own choice, but by the will of the one who subjected it, in hope that the creation itself will be liberated from its bondage to decay and brought into the freedom and glory of the children of God (Rom. 8:20-21, NIV).

We, like the disciples, must expand our vision of the kingdom of God to be as glorious as the marred creation around us knows it will be.

We must look for tangible manifestations of the rule of Christ in our lives, homes and churches – even as we look for His plunder of this world through our vocational assignments. But as we do, may we not shrink the kingdom of God down to the size of our own personal experiences and relationships. No! "For you have not come to what may be touched…" (Heb. 12:18).

The mystery of the gospel and of the kingdom of God is that by faith we have Christ in us the hope of glory (Col. 1:27)! We have the power of the Spirit of God who resurrected Christ from the dead living within us as the guarantee of every promise of God (Rom. 8:11; 2 Cor. 1:22)! We are participants in a kingdom that *not only* cannot be shaken, but it must not be shrunk (Heb. 12:28). Jesus, the King of kings and Lord of all creation brought the kingdom of heaven down to earth, defeated sin and death, only to ascend back to His Father. The prophet Daniel records his vision of the reuniting:

Behold, with the clouds of heaven
   there came one like a son of man,

And he came to the Ancient of Days
   and was presented before him.
And to him was given dominion
   and glory and a kingdom,
that all peoples, nations, and languages
   should serve him;
his dominion is an everlasting dominion,
   which shall not pass away,
and his kingdom one
   that shall not be destroyed.
(Dan. 7:13-14)

Daniel's vision is not merely a hope for the future. Reflecting on the affect of the resurrection, the apostle Paul declares it a reality. Jesus is currently reigning at the right hand of the Father.

Then comes the end, when he delivers the kingdom to God the Father after destroying every rule and every authority and power. For he must reign until he has put all his enemies under his feet (1 Cor. 15:24-25).

This is the scope of the kingdom of God that has come to earth in Christ and will endure forever. This is the kingdom into which ministers of the gospel are vocationally called to serve as ambassadors of Christ, until He returns. We must not forget this, regardless of our model of ministry and assigned sphere of influence. It is bigger.

If God has given you a vision of ministry that includes His material provision for your life by means of tentmaking or multiple vocations that are both inside and outside of His church – contextualize your call inside of a grander vision of

His plunderous kingdom! The kingdom of heaven is at hand, and this impacts and informs everything to which you put your hands. Certainly, you must consider the scriptural merits, contextual complexities, realistic costs, missional benefits and personal "fit" of the model, but do not fixate on them. Place your vision of vocational faithfulness within a larger vision of God's sovereign faithfulness to bring His kingdom down to earth in Jesus through His church, by His Spirit, within His people. Do so with urgency, expectation and hopefulness. And as you do, audibly add your voice to the myriad of voices that John heard in heaven: "The kingdom of the world has become the kingdom of our Lord and of his Christ, and he shall reign forever and ever" (Rev. 11.15).

THE SACRED AND THE SECULAR?

It is easy for the bi-vocational or tentmaking minister to feel as though they have their feet planted in two different worlds, the sacred and the secular. Throughout this work, I have semantically described it as such. This may be what it feels like, but is it an accurate depiction of reality?

The Scriptures undeniably present a distinct, practical and eternal division between those who are set against the Lord and His anointed, and those who find refuge in Him (Ps. 2). There is a battle between the two. Paul elaborates:

> Put on the whole armor of God, that you may be able to stand against the schemes of the devil. For we do not wrestle against flesh and blood, but against the rulers, against the authorities, against the cosmic powers over this present darkness, against the spiritual forces of evil in the heavenly places (Eph. 6:11-12).

We must acknowledge that there is a sacredness, holiness and set-apartness to the people of God who have experienced His saving grace and who take refuge in Christ. Truly there *is* a divide between the righteous and the wicked. There are people whose hearts have been changed from death to life, from corrupt to cleansed – and there are those whose hearts have not. Jesus Himself confirms that there are good and evil people in the world. "Out of the abundance of the heart the mouth speaks. The good person out of his good treasure brings forth good, and the evil person out of his evil treasure brings forth evil" (Matt. 12:34-35). If it is out of the heart that the mouth speaks, then it is out of the heart that plans are formed, businesses are launched, teams are managed, classes are taught, etc. In a world with good and evil hearts, there will be good and evil places, governments, corporations, schools, and other entities. There will be a sacred and a secular.

And yet, whenever God strategically sends and assigns His servants to represent His kingdom within the kingdoms of this world, the very fact of our assignment evidences that there is not a total divide between the sacred and the secular. He has sent us. It is His world, under His feet, awaiting His return, culminating in His end!

Bi-vocational or tentmaking minister, live your life inside of this truth. Engage your vocational duality with a singular, undivided reality. Your life is His. Your redemption is His. Your time is His. Your gifts are His. The world is His. The plunder is His. Boast in the Lord, your vocational paradigm is His.

> Teach me your way, O Lord,
>   that I may walk in your truth;
> unite my heart to fear your name.
> (Psalm 86:11)

A final word of encouragement from a tentmaking servant who deserves the last word:

Grace to you and peace from God our Father and the Lord Jesus Christ.

Blessed be the God and Father of our Lord Jesus Christ, who has blessed us in Christ with every spiritual blessing in the heavenly places, even as he chose us in him before the foundation of the world, that we should be holy and blameless before him. In love he predestined us for adoption to himself as sons through Jesus Christ, according to the purpose of his will, to the praise of his glorious grace, with which he has blessed us in the Beloved. In him we have redemption through his blood, the forgiveness of our trespasses, according to the riches of his grace, which he lavished upon us, in all wisdom and insight making known to us the mystery of his will, according to his purpose, which he set forth in Christ as a plan for the fullness of time, to unite all things in him, things in heaven and things on earth.

In him we have obtained an inheritance, having been predestined according to the purpose of him who works all things according to the counsel of his will, so that we who were the first to hope in Christ might be to the praise of his glory. In him you also, when you heard the word of truth, the gospel of your salvation, and believed in him, were sealed with the promised Holy Spirit, who is the guarantee of our inheritance until we acquire possession of it, to the praise of his glory. Amen.

Also available from Christian Focus ...

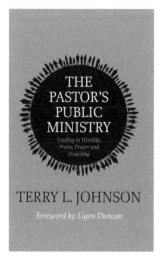

978-1-5271-1164-6

The Pastor's Public Ministry

Leading in Worship, Praise, Prayer and Preaching

Terry L. Johnson

Ministers, in our age, are expected to be jacks–of–all–trades. However important administration, committee work, counselling, and relationship building may be, the pastor's public ministry in the preaching of the Word and leading of public worship and prayer are fundamental.

The Bible lays out specific qualifications for elders and deacon. The gospel is guarded by requiring those who hold public office to have high standards of knowledge, character, and conduct. Terry Johnson lays out that, if this is true for "lay" leadership, how much more important for those called to ministry.

Christian Focus Publications

Our mission statement
Staying Faithful

In dependence upon God we seek to impact the world through literature faithful to His infallible Word, the Bible. Our aim is to ensure that the Lord Jesus Christ is presented as the only hope to obtain forgiveness of sin, live a useful life and look forward to heaven with Him.

Our Books are published in four imprints:

◁○▷ CHRISTIAN FOCUS

Popular works including biographies, commentaries, basic doctrine and Christian living.

◁○▷ MENTOR

Books written at a level suitable for Bible College and seminary students, pastors, and other serious readers. The imprint includes commentaries, doctrinal studies, examination of current issues and church history.

◁○▷ CHRISTIAN HERITAGE

Books representing some of the best material from the rich heritage of the church.

◁○▷ CF4KIDS

Children's books for quality Bible teaching and for all age groups: Sunday school curriculum, puzzle and activity books; personal and family devotional titles, biographies and inspirational stories – because you are never too young to know Jesus!

Christian Focus Publications Ltd,
Geanies House, Fearn, Ross-shire,
IV20 1TW, Scotland, United Kingdom.
www.christianfocus.com